THE ALAMO DELEGATE

THE ODYSSEY OF JESSE B. BADGETT

ALBERT LYTLE PARTEE

THE ONTEORA PRESS

To my brother,
Robert Padgett Partee
(1963-2017)

CONTENTS

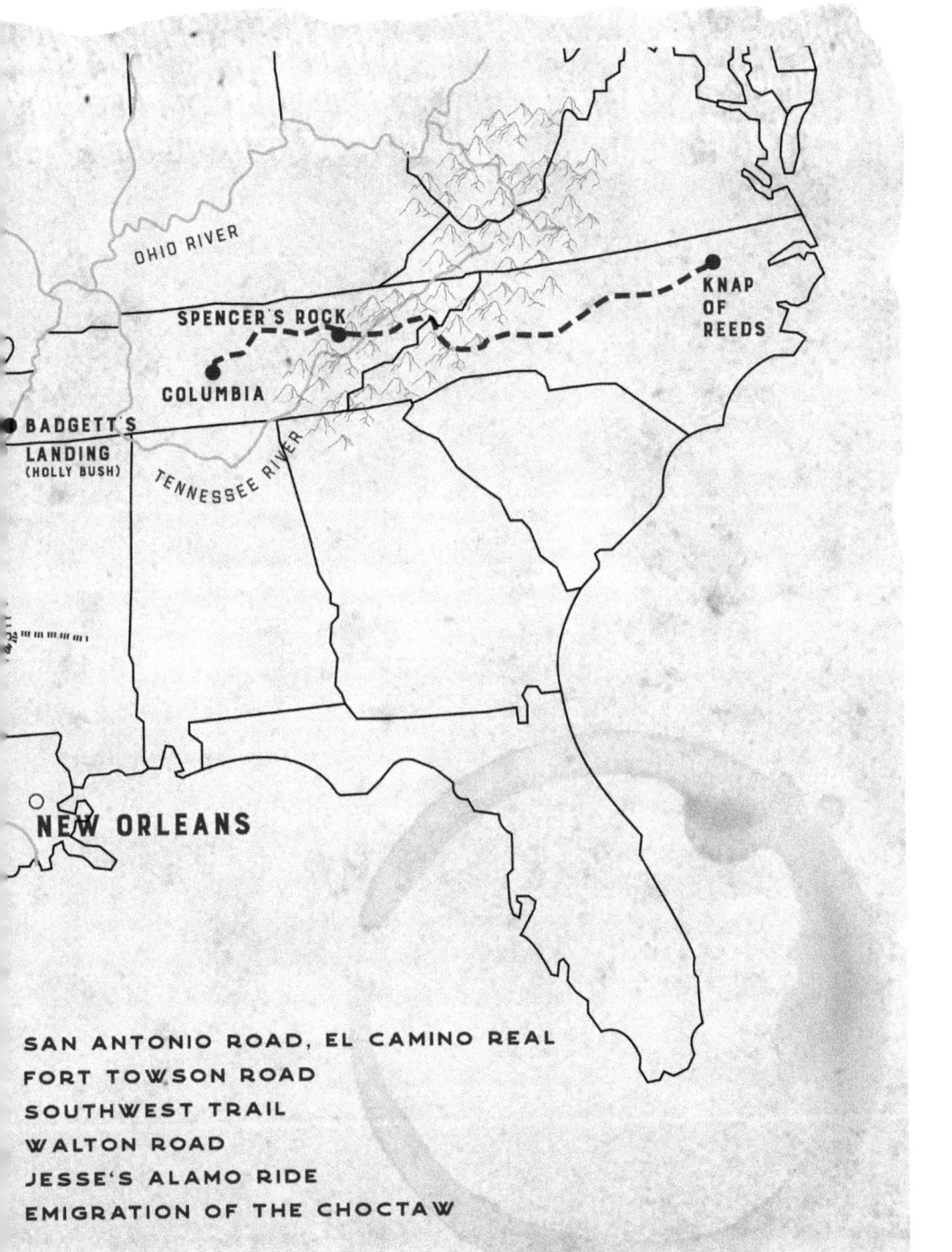

OHIO RIVER

SPENCER'S ROCK

KNAP
OF
REEDS

COLUMBIA

BADGETT'S
LANDING
(HOLLY BUSH)

TENNESSEE RIVER

NEW ORLEANS

SAN ANTONIO ROAD, EL CAMINO REAL
FORT TOWSON ROAD
SOUTHWEST TRAIL
WALTON ROAD
JESSE'S ALAMO RIDE
EMIGRATION OF THE CHOCTAW

PART I

1

COLUMBIA

Whil hen six-year-old Jesse B. Badgett passed through Knoxville, Tennessee, in the early spring of 1813, the year was just starting to lose its chill. Charles Partee, his grandfather, led Jesse and his extended family from North Carolina's Coastal Plain to Tennessee, where they would settle.

They were among the many who forged westward past the Great Smoky Mountains, seeking more and better land on which to build their lives. While the transmontane land was still being surveyed, reports told of deep, rich soil and abundant waterways, ideal for animal husbandry. The land would also be ideal for farming—especially cotton, the production of which had doubled every year since the turn of the century. Cotton was a business that could make a family comfortably rich within a decade.

Leaving their old homes on Knap of Reeds Creek in Granville County, they traveled up Jonesboro Road to Knoxville in a family caravan of horses and wagons. Charles led the way with his three youngest children, Jesse's uncles and aunt, including the sixteen-year-old Claney, fourteen-year-old Hiram, and Sally, who was only twelve. Close behind them, Charles's newly-married eldest son, Locker, escorted his pregnant wife, Marcia. Jesse walked alongside his parents: his grandfather's middle daughter, Levina—"Viney"—and her husband, Benton Badgett.[1]

Two winters prior, Charles had accompanied his son Abner's family, along with several enslaved people, to begin work on a beautiful 1,800-acre tract where Knob Creek empties into the Duck River in Maury County, Tennessee. His land had plenty of fresh water, including the creek, a long stretch of the Duck's right bank, and a cool freshwater spring. Relatively flat, it beckoned to be cleared and cultivated. This tract was the remainder of the five thousand acres granted to Charles as compensation for assisting the North Carolina militia during the Revolution. After selling off 3,200 acres, he had had enough cash to locate and survey the land, with some money left over for moving expenses. Once in Tennessee, he directed the clearing of land, the planting of crops, and the raising of suitable buildings to receive most of his household.[2]

The following winter, in 1812, just over a year before Jesse's family trudged westward, Charles had returned to Granville County. He had tended to some business before returning to Tennessee along with more of his family and many of the enslaved people he had originally left behind to continue work in North Carolina.

Finally, Charles came for Jesse and the rest of the family, leaving behind only his son Arkey, who would stay to work the Granville County land. Charles knew well the journey's requirements. Still, there were no easy days for Jesse, as traveling in such a large group—three households and the enslaved people who accompanied them—demanded slow, careful progress. They rose with the sun, or just before it, to break camp and begin their daily trek. As the eldest of the Badgett children, Jesse was expected to keep an eye on his five younger siblings. The task sometimes permitted him to ride at the front of the fore wagon, but only when he held his little brother Samuel still and quiet in his lap. With Samuel, this was possible. Jesse's other brothers, Noah and William, on the other hand, largely regarded stillness as unnatural and wicked. But Samuel could be convinced to sit on Jesse's lap in the seat next to their grandfather. From this vantage point, they could see the road ahead.

Because his eyes were better than his grandfather's, Jesse was the first to spot the sharp rooftop of the old, abandoned blockhouse at Fort Southwest Point. The building sat outside Kingston on a knoll that overlooked the confluence of the rivers Clinch and Tennessee. The sight came with some relief to their party, as it marked the starting place of the Walton Road, their path for about a hundred and thirty miles to Nashville, passing roughly through Crossville, Monterey, Cookeville, Carthage, and Gallatin. Up to fifteen feet wide, the road was leveled from the sides of the hills, with bridges and ferries to make water crossings easier and safer. The men hoped they could keep a pace of twelve to fifteen miles a day on this road.

However, once they passed the fort, they would need to traverse the Cumberland Plateau. The thousand-foot-high plateau was difficult to ascend, and there was a risk of losing an over-burdened wagon to its steep slope. By carrying as much as they could on foot, they could lessen the risk that, upon approaching the top of the plateau, everything would tumble back down. They camped one night at the bottom of the rise and spent the next night at the top, exhausted.

Walton Road snaked through a winding, wooded valley for the next two days' travel. Hard-packed, it had been cleared of stumps, but the curves and the hills and the trees made it difficult to see far ahead. On the third day, the road seemed to have reached its apex when they came to a stop at the foot of a natural stone monolith.

His father, Benton, explained that this was Spencer's Rock, a landmark they had been told was twenty-five miles down the road from the fort. Jesse was fascinated by this outcropping which stood out alone against the side of the hill. Lined with creases and cracks, it resembled wrinkles on an old, wizened face.

By agreement, at the end of each grueling day, Jesse would grab his slate and run back to meet his father at their family wagon. Benton had attached a device to the rear wheel. Purchased back in North Carolina, the wooden box contained a series of numbered cogs. Every four hundred turns of the wagon wheel, the counter would click forward to the next number, showing the miles they had traveled that day.

Benton had anxiously justified the purchase to his father-in-law before they set out, knowing that the device would attract the older man's attention. He had gotten quite the deal, he claimed, because it was heavily used, the cogs worn such that it had to be reset before it could reach mile eighteen. Still, it would suit their purpose fine. It had been used by a surveyor on his explorations of the area they were traveling through, Benton added, so the measurements should match his notes. His mouth pressed into a thin, skeptical line, Charles had examined the device as Benton explained how it worked. Most of their way would be marked with mileposts every five miles, so the older man saw little value in the thing. Jesse suspected that the real reason his father had bought it was the reason he gave only to Jesse— that it was modeled after one invented and used by Benjamin Franklin.

At the foot of Spencer's Rock, they read the numbered box and found that it showed eight miles that day. Jesse wrote the figure on his slate, adding it to the previous day's progress. They found twenty-six total miles. Jesse asked if they should write to tell the surveyor of his error, which made Benton laugh and say that they should consider it.

"Why is it called Spencer's Rock?" Jesse asked.

"I understand a man called 'Big Foot' Spencer lived in a tree near here. He was killed by the Cherokee." Seeing Jesse's face turn a shade paler, Benton added, "But that was twenty years ago, son. We have the area under more control now."

When they set off the next day, the road followed a steep downhill grade. They proceeded carefully to avoid losing their wagons until, finally, the land began to flatten out. With the last of the hills behind them, the sky stretched out forever, meeting the horizon at what seemed an impossible distance away.

The youngest Badgett, one-year-old Elvira, had taken to hollering as soon as they began to move each morning. Jesse could hardly understand why she would stir up such a noise. He thought that if their positions had been reversed and he could make the journey in the comfort of his mother's arms, then he would spend the days sleeping.

"Why does she yell so much?" Jesse mumbled to his grandfather. "Seems like she would be more comfortable if she would quiet herself."

Charles shrugged. "Babes that young do not understand about the passing discomfort of travel. Things are harder for them that do not understand."

Jesse adjusted Samuel in his lap and considered this.

"Did you cry like that on the ship?"

Jesse had been told that his grandfather Charles had been born in Versailles, France, and crossed the Atlantic Ocean as a child with his parents. Charles gave him the bemused look he always did when Jesse asked him questions that could have no sensible answers.

"I suppose I may have put up a racket, but I surely do not remember." He nodded toward Elvira, still squalling behind them. "She will not remember this trip, either. Once we settle in, it will quickly seem for her, and perhaps little Samuel, too, as if we had always been there."

Jesse nodded, considering. "Will I remember?"

Charles grunted but gave no other answer, and Jesse knew this meant that he should stop asking questions. An unsmiling man, his grandfather's demeanor said more than his words. The boy saw how the adults deferred to Charles, calling him "colonel" in his presence and "the old man" in his absence.

Jesse called him "grandfather" sometimes but, more often, simply "sir."

He considered his unanswered question, deciding that he could not possibly forget how the sky had opened up a little more each day. He might forget his soreness or how he longed for the familiar comfort of their lives back in North Carolina. There were trials each day, and the road tossed up snags at them from time to time like a spiteful animal.

But he would always remember how it felt to set their backs to the rising sun and watch as it lit the whole, wide country before them.

As spring advanced, she brought with her warmth and storms. The more challenging weather forced them to stop and shelter in the wagons, huddled and crammed together with their heads down. After these storms, the road, which revealed more neglect the farther west they traveled, grew slick with mud and impassable. They tried to take advantage of these forced pauses after storms, hunting and making repairs as they waited for the road to dry and harden, but Charles grew impatient. Moisture saturated the air so that the road was stubborn against drying even in the bright sun. On one of these days, Charles insisted they set off on the soft road. They would go slowly, but at least they would make progress. Benton gently advised that they wait until after noon, but Locker sided with his father, so the group pushed forward.

Jesse took his place on the wagon seat with Samuel in his lap. They had been moving at a crawl for not more than an hour when the wagon jerked to a stop, nearly jostling the baby out of his arms. The horses protested. The driver urged them forward once, but, seeing how their effort only managed to tilt the wagon rather than move it forward, Charles called a halt and climbed to the ground, his boots sinking through the mud to the rock below. With progress stalled, the men quickly joined the old man to examine the cause of the delay. Brothers William and Noah soon appeared, eager to join any action, as Jesse struggled to climb down with Samuel in tow.

At first, it was not clear what was hindering the wagon wheel. Charles told his driver to dig into the mud to expose the problem. Obeying, the man discovered an oddly shaped rock with a cleft that held the wagon wheel fast. Jesse felt a hand on his shoulder, and his father was there, steadying himself as he bent to look. A moment later, his mother appeared, too. Jesse struggled to hold a squirming Samuel, and Viney called for help from Betsy and fifteen-year-old Elsie, enslaved people who had been with the Badgett family for as long as Jesse could remember. His mother passed Elvira into Elsie's arms while Betsy took Samuel.

Rocking the wagon back and forth, the men tried to free the wheel from the crack, but it seemed irrevocably stuck. The muddy ground around the rock would not give the traction needed to escape the obstacle. Soon, an argument ensued on how to continue. Charles suddenly cursed and called for a hammer, insisting that they break up the rock.

Benton moved to the rear of the wagon where the tools were kept, and for a moment, everyone believed he was following the instruction. But instead of a hammer, he pulled one of the long, tough wooden poles that were stored on the undercarriage. Charles narrowed his eyes at him but did not speak as Benton suggested that they simply use a lever to lift the wheel out of the cleft, allowing the wagon to move forward.

Charles frowned at him but gestured that they could go ahead and try.

"Stand ready to lead the horses forward," Benton ordered the driver. "On my word." Then, he knelt and wedged the end of the pole between the wheel and the rock's cleft. He told three men to grasp the end of the pole and prepare to lift the wheel.

On Benton's command, the men strained against the pole, managing a small movement upward. Just as the wheel caught on the top of the rock, Benton shouted, "Pull her forward."

The horses strained for a couple of seconds as Jesse and his brothers watched, holding their breath. There was a startling *crack* as several things happened at once: the wheel gained the lift it needed to roll over the rock's lip, it lurched up and over onto the other side, and the pole snapped off at the end, leaving it shorter and splintered.

Jesse's mother moved to observe their progress and looked on with affection for her husband. Her gentle smile faded when her gaze moved up to her father's face.

"Oh, Papa," she protested at his frown, "Better the pole than the wheel."

Charles gave no indication of hearing but rather quietly climbed back onto the wagon's bench, signaling to everyone that it was time to resume the day's forward progress.

Fortunately, a stuck wheel and a broken pole were among the worst of their troubles on that long journey. As the summer solstice approached, the days grew longer and hotter. The terrain descended from the Cumberland Plateau to the Highland Rim and finally to the

Central Basin, in which lay their new land. On good days, they pushed fifteen miles forward. More often, they crawled ahead only six or seven miles. Sometimes, they made no progress at all. Finally, they reached the Duck River, glittering and green in the afternoon sun, and began to follow its meandering course through the countryside.

On June 16, 1813, they found the place where Knob Creek met the river. They had arrived at their destination. Uncle Abner, who had been watching for some weeks, met them eagerly on horseback. He seemed to ride out of the setting sun that blazed in front of them like a beacon. As Abner dismounted to embrace and greet them, they paused, but soon they resumed their progress, riding together to the cleared patch of land outside a town named Columbia, on which stood the structures that would serve as their new home.[3]

2

WAVERLEY

By July of 1822, Jesse had grown into a young man of fifteen. He tried to stand tall, the way he had seen his father do. But as Benton was lowered into the ground, he felt every bit a boy. Jesse knew that only children whined about death's unfairness, so he kept such thoughts to himself.[1]

Since he was too young to claim his inheritance, it would be administered by his mother under the supervision of the county probate court until he came of legal age at twenty-one—a lifetime away, in Jesse's estimation. Now, there were debts to be settled, and his father's personal property would be sold at auction to raise money for their living expenses and the estate's operation.

Jesse missed his father. He frequently heard that he favored Benton, even more often since the man's untimely passing. He did not know if this was properly true or simply a thing people said. Sometimes, he heard his father's voice in his own, the echo of some meter or cadence or phrasing that he had unconsciously learned from him. Though he was scarcely aware of it, he also shared his father's habit of walking with his hands clasped behind his back.

With Jesse's help, his mother kept the inventory and accounts and presided over an auction later that month. Displayed in a line by the barn, the family's plows looked like soldiers, uncomfortable in their new and unnatural formation. Neighbors and family attended the event, along with a couple of strangers attracted by the announcement. They milled around the grounds and filtered in and out of the house. As he moved through his own home, Jesse could feel their eyes flitting from him to the family's possessions. No longer simply things used in the course of the family's daily routine, the items suddenly held commercial value. They seemed different now that they were offered for sale to the highest bidder. He felt sure that, out of respect for Benton's eldest son, others would hang back and let him make his choices before they stepped forward to make bids for the remainder.

He smiled sadly as he first selected a saddle. Here was one point where he and his father differed. Though Benton had, of course, been a competent rider, Jesse had taken to riding as other boys took to walking. He was fast and fearless on horseback. It was this skill primarily that afforded him the money to buy the saddle from the estate sale, as he had acted in recent years as a courier or hired hand whenever he could. Scarce at the time, coins were a rare and valuable form of payment. Most times, he accepted goods such as eggs, salt, lard, and whatever else his neighbors offered up for bargaining. Some of these items he kept for his family's use, but he sold what he could. As he grew better known in the wider area, he was able to make some small trades. Still underage, he was not yet trusted with larger, speculative exchanges for which he could not be legally obligated, but he was increasingly liked and trusted among the local planters and traders.

Along with various tools he wanted to keep for use on their farm, he wanted his father's umbrella, shot bag, and books. Benton had taught him to read not just his letters but, as he grew into a young man, to study words and their uses. Jesse shared his father's respect for literary effort, and the memory of Benton's reading voice would not allow him to part with his father's books. He also planned to take it upon himself to continue the education of his younger siblings, particularly William, Noah, and Samuel. His mother, who knew many things except how to read and write, would instruct his sisters, Mary and Elvira. As he gathered his selections, he raised his head, inadvertently catching his grandfather's eye.

Charles frowned. Seeing he had Jesse's attention, he made a gesture that Jesse knew well—a simple backward jerk of the head that meant, *Come here, boy.*

Jesse hesitated before he obeyed. He felt sure that he knew what Charles's counsel would be, and he knew, too, his own response. But opening with rudeness would do nothing in his favor.

Tension had grown between his parents and his grandfather in the years before Benton's death. Charles imagined himself a benevolent feudal lord, owning the land and some enslaved people. He was, in his mind, the center of everything and everyone he knew. After leaving North Carolina, they had all pooled their efforts toward the greater good of the family. They had developed the land to make their living and grown cotton as a cash crop. Five years into the project, Benton had insisted that he own the land he worked and, in 1818, he bought 100 acres from his father-in-law for $500.00. This made the Badgetts less dependent upon the old man. Yet, the four years that followed before Benton died were too short a time for the Badgetts to do much more than sustain themselves.[2]

Since coming to Tennessee, they understood more clearly that they were not full members of the Partee clan because Charles favored the sons of his house over his daughters. Though Locker had died shortly after arriving in Tennessee, his brothers Abner, Claney, Hiram, and Arkey all lived on the old man's Maury County land. Only Noah stayed in North Carolina on a plantation in Rowan County among his wife's people.

Though Levina spent many days visiting Charles in his home, she could not close the gaps that had opened between them, and she acutely felt the distance between herself and her father and brothers. Her family had come with him to Tennessee, and she had been respectful and dutiful, but Charles seemed impossible to satisfy.

First catching his mother's eye to indicate the items he was setting aside, Jesse answered Charles's silent summons by clasping his hands behind his back and moving around the table and across the room to his grandfather.

The old man did not speak at first, and Jesse began to wonder if he should initiate the conversation. Finally, Charles said, "Son, what are you intending?"

"I intend to purchase some of my pa's things," Jesse replied, keeping his voice on a steady keel. He could confidently ride a galloping horse with no fear of stumbling, but, especially when speaking with his grandfather, he preferred to parcel his words with careful control and deliberation.

"With what?" Charles asked.

Jesse was tempted to quip "with coin of the realm," but he knew that would be no better than rudeness. Charles found no amusement in verbal dodges, so the younger man tried to address what he thought was his grandfather's underlying question. "I believe I have sufficient money for a few things at a reasonable price. As you know, I have worked a good deal this past year and made a few good trades."

"And some poor ones," Charles countered.

Jesse shrugged and gestured the comment away before returning his hands behind his back. "As it goes. On balance, good."

This was only partially true, and Jesse hoped that the old man would not question him. If outright asked, he would have to choose whether to lie or admit that some—but only a minor part—of his available money was borrowed. Recently, fewer and fewer men would take cotton as payment for goods, as its value was little compared to its weight, and there were other things easier to move on one's own. This meant those who had only cotton to spare were growing more willing to part with it on speculation. Jesse had managed to secure a small shipment of cotton in this way, so part of the money he held secure in a folded square of canvas was owed elsewhere. Still, Jesse was confident that he could make up the difference later.

Charles considered him with narrowed eyes, setting his mouth in a familiar, thin line. In this relatively public space among his family and neighbors, he would not raise his voice or declare his disapproval.

"I concede a saddle of your own," Charles said, nodding. "But you may do your family better service and secure our profits if you did not spend much."

Privately, Jesse bristled at Charles's use of the plural *our profits*. He thought his grandfather a skinflint.

"I agree, sir," Jesse said aloud.

"Arkey tells me you have talked about acquiring a cotton gin."

"Yes, sir."

Uncle Arkey had also suggested—but had not promised—that his family would help build a cotton gin for Jesse, provided, of course, that they could make full use of it for their own crops. Jesse said nothing of this to Charles.

"Perhaps consider luxuries for a time after such plans are completed."

Jesse nodded, affirming, "I will consider all purchases carefully, sir."

Charles gave him the nod that indicated his dismissal, and the young man returned to the corner table where he had left his selected items. Considering, Jesse replaced a coffee urn but kept the stack of his father's books. He picked up a well-thumbed copy of *Waverley*. He rubbed his thumb along the spine and remembered how his father read to him the stories of chivalric deeds and lost causes until he gained the literacy to read it back, often by firelight in the winter evenings. With some deliberation, he placed it on the stack with ten other titles he intended to purchase. He did not raise his head to meet Charles's eye again.[3]

Shortly after the estate auction, Jesse was obligated by law to work for the public overseer on the county road near his home, a road that ran from the ford of the creek at Witherspoon's place to the crossroads on the Columbia side of his grandfather's land. At first, he had resented the time spent away from his business endeavors. It was October, the days were growing shorter, and harvest's end grew ever closer. Nevertheless, he understood the reason for the work and believed in its necessity.

His hard work had already molded his stature into that of a

sturdy, muscular man. The road was some twelve feet wide and had to be regularly cleared and compacted to carry the heavily laden, rolling stock of local farmers. Remembering the trouble the roads had given them when leaving North Carolina, Jesse took this responsibility to heart. He also liked the way the road—straighter than was possible in the eastern hills and mountains—cut through the land and joined up with other roads, imposing order on the landscape.[4]

Many of the nearby landowners found ways to avoid road work. They hired substitutes or sent field hands to act in their stead. It was from these men Jesse learned a great many things about the nearby farms and plantations. Most of all, he grew to understand their needs —what each lacked and what each had in surplus. The men also spoke of the flatboats that traveled to New Orleans, following the Duck River to the Cumberland, then the Ohio, and finally the Mississippi. Some carried shipments of produce bound for eastern markets. Others brought manufactured goods down the Ohio from Cincinnati. A docked boat, Jesse learned, was a trove of opportunity for news and trade.

Among the many bits of news, Jesse heard the story of a farmer downriver who had purchased a cotton gin stand that would soon be delivered and assembled. He had concocted a justification for visiting the farm but soon found that no excuse was necessary. Several other boys and young men from the locality wanted to investigate the gin as well. Upon making the trip, Jesse saw that the machine, manufactured in Massachusetts, was smaller than he had expected. He knew a gin stand could process fifty pounds of cotton each day—fifty times that of two enslaved workers operating by hand—and he had naively pictured a device the size of the wagon that brought them from North Carolina. In fact, in his estimation, it was only three feet wide. Its strong wooden frame sat on four legs like a table. On one side of its boxed frame protruded a large iron wheel crank with a handle. On the other, a slanted receiving chute disgorged into a large opening, spitting its wares into a collection basket.

"Manufactured in Massachusetts," the farmer explained, pleased with his audience. He obliged their curiosity by raising the lid to reveal the gin's inner workings. The crank turned a long, metal wheel —the largest single piece of metal that Jesse had ever seen—with many fine hooked teeth. Demonstrating with a basket of unprocessed cotton, the farmer showed how the teeth pulled the cotton through the mesh, leaving behind the seeds. Jesse quickly realized that the machine could indeed be scaled much larger than the modest device he observed.

"Do stands like this come any larger?" Jesse asked. When the farmer did not answer, the young man looked up from the workings of the gin and saw the man frowning at him. "My apologies. I am merely curious. It is a fine machine."

The farmer shrugged. "I am certain they do. I hear plantations in Georgia are building gins that take up whole barns, but this will suit me. At least for a few years."

Jesse considered this carefully as he rode back to his homestead. When he had told Charles that he would consider his purchases carefully, he meant it. And such a machine—sufficient for cleaning a single small farm's harvest production—was smaller than the kind he would need.

3

A LAND OF OPPORTUNITY

J esse stood quietly, gazing out the front window in the lobby of William E. Woodruff's office, the intellectual heart of Little Rock's *Arkansas Gazette*. Shifting uncomfortably in the muggy afternoon heat, he half-listened to his brother William talk with Woodruff and the others about the politics of the Arkansas Territory. He liked the capital city best when the streets were quiet, as they were that warm, still afternoon. Sometimes, he missed Columbia. There were fewer people here, but Little Rock's political intrigues meant the city was growing, bringing more activity to the territory's hub.[1]

The increased activity meant opportunity. For one thing, Jesse and William had taken work in town as store clerks. The two had different strengths: William had a fine head for figures and good leadership traits, and Jesse had a knack for keeping track of people's needs. His skill on a horse, too, meant he was often on the site of a potential sale or steamboat arrival.[2]

There were other opportunities, too. Working in town, Jesse and William found themselves minor witnesses to the local political drama.

Based upon what they had seen and heard the week before—July

20, 1831—the Badgett brothers had agreed to attach their names to a statement that Woodruff would publish as an extra to the *Gazette* that day as fast as the enslaved worker could work the printing press. The piece supported Chester Ashley, a political friend of Woodruff's, in an election dispute between him and Colonel Ambrose H. Sevier. Despite their names appearing on the statement, the matter did not affect them, so Jesse's mind was elsewhere. The Badgetts were the central figures of legal troubles back in Tennessee, and his thoughts drifted there.[3]

In the nearly ten years since their father's death, the Badgetts had been beset by bad luck and family disputes, leading them to leave Maury County—and Tennessee altogether—to make a new life in the Arkansas Territory.[4] It had taken several years before Jesse achieved his goal of building a cotton gin. When the Jesse B. Badgett Cotton Gin was fully operational in 1827, it facilitated, for a time, the business he had first promised himself after his father's death. He bought his stand, not from faraway Massachusetts, but from Georgia. The machine now ran on the second floor of a building he had constructed on his family's Tennessee property while the land was still held in probate. Since the gin was housed so near the road, a terrain he knew well from his service on the public works crew, the gin was easily accessible to accept cotton from nearby farms, including the homeplaces of his grandfather and his uncles Abner, Arkey, and Claney. The only notable exclusion was his Uncle Hiram, who had moved to Gibson County, Tennessee, in 1818.[5]

He had been right in his suspicions that a cotton gin was easily scaled. Placed upon a sixty-saw stand, six feet wide and fifteen feet long, the gin was powered by mules that turned the running gear from the first floor. Next to the building sat a baling press, which he was sure his father would have found fascinating. Set atop a large screw hewn from a log about twenty feet high, a pyramid-structured roof stood tall. Two beams led away from the pyramid at an angle, carefully weighted to balance one another so that a horse or mule could pull one in a circle and rotate the screw down into the press, forming three- to five-hundred-pound bales of dense cotton fiber, which could be bound in hemp netting and sold.[6]

Life slowly got tougher for the Badgetts after thirty-two-year-old Arkey moved permanently to Maury County in the fall of 1820. Since 1813, Arkey had independently worked the old man's farm back in Granville County before the place was sold. On his own so far from Charles, Arkey quickly grew accustomed to getting his own way.

In his dotage, Charles became more intemperate in his habits, drinking hard apple cider every day. The old man seemed to harden with each passing year, his resentments and grievances growing deeper, as did the wrinkles on his face.

Uncle Arkey had prospered on his own in North Carolina, but he carried a restless and insatiable appetite that drove him to acquire greater control over his father's affairs. When he gained control over anything or anyone, he had a strong aversion to relaxing his hold. He exercised his influence over Charles at every opportunity, always with the aim of keeping a tight rein on his father's assets, even if it meant cruelty to his sister and her family.

The trouble started for the Badgetts when Arkey went to court and charged Jesse and Viney with the unlawful detainer of Elsie and her three children. This came as a shock for Jesse and his mother. Jesse had known Elsie all his life. She had come to Tennessee with them, and the Badgett household had depended upon her labor and that of her children.[7]

Three years prior, there had been work to do, and Elsie had gone to stay for a few years at Charles's homeplace, moving next to Arkey's separate 350-acre farm. Shortly after Elsie and her family returned to the Badgetts, Arkey demanded them right back. The Badgetts resisted as they considered Elsie to be long since given to them and their need for her the greater.

Arkey won the lawsuit. There was no paperwork to memorialize the gift, and Charles and Arkey agreed in court that Elsie had only ever been on loan to the Badgetts. Levina pleaded with her father, but her petition was met with Charles's silent dismissal.

After Arkey obtained a court order in 1827 for Elsie, the local magistrates arrived at the Badgett place with a search warrant. They were to find her and turn her over to Arkey. Confronting the officers of the law, Jesse turned them away at the point of a pistol. The Badgetts appealed the court order.

The tensions between Uncle Arkey and Jesse had escalated dangerously.

Arkey's avarice soon caused more trouble for Jesse. In 1828, Arkey was sued by the partnership of Dick, Booker, and Company, who claimed that he had knowingly sold the firm bales of cotton that were fraudulently weighted in the center with bracken and trash. It was becoming a common grift to gin cotton free of seeds and debris and then, as it was being loaded into the press, fill what would become the center of the bale with heavy trash. Fine, clean fiber was then packed around the refuse. The bale would be beautiful and evenly white all the way around, and wherever it was tested, even three to five inches deep, the buyer would find only excellent, usable fiber. It was not until well into processing that the truth was revealed: the bale contained far less cotton than was paid for and, already partially processed, could not be easily returned.

Jesse knew that Arkey left parts of his field to be reaped too late, when it was harder to clear the lint from the stem, and frequently delivered his harvest to the gin still wet. In this state, lint could not be properly ginned, and it could damage the internal drum and cogs. Jesse did not know if Arkey would sink so low as to instruct his hands to weight the bales with trash, but he could not be sure, so he did not know if the buyers were taking advantage of the situation or had a genuine complaint. Regardless, Jesse had been prepared to stand for the quality of any cotton coming from his gin when news came that Arkey had already replied to the lawsuit. His uncle alleged that any fraud was squarely and solely the doing of Jesse and Noah Badgett.

Less than a year after he reached the age of twenty-one and could properly claim his inheritance, the repute of Jesse's operation was soiled, his credit was ruined, and those who held debts in his name were impatient for repayment. Counting on his inheritance, Jesse had relied, perhaps overmuch, on credit and speculation to operate, and now he found himself nearly insolvent.[8]

The final straw came when the old man died one winter night in 1829.

When Jesse returned home from the gin, he found his mother seated at the table, attempting to mend a dark blue skirt that had snagged on a nail and torn. Jesse did not notice her distress until she cried out after pricking her hand with the needle. Levina was not one to be careless or to yelp at a prick, so Jesse came to see. In her unusual haste and distemper, she had slipped the needle clear across her palm. Jesse looked at her hand and found that, though she was not bleeding, her hands shook terribly.

"What has happened, Ma?"

Viney took a slow, shuddering breath and explained that the inevitable had come to pass. Charles had died in his sleep the night before. With a grave nod, Jesse offered appropriate prayers for his departed soul. Levina bowed her head but, still trembling, did not share in his amen.

"Arkey came with the news, and he...reported on Papa's will. He seemed quite victorious. Papa had it drawn up by Will Kennedy, undoubtedly under Arkey's influence, and has left us barely enough to survive. He went as far as to..." Levina stopped to swallow, steadying her voice. "As to support in writing your Uncle Arkey in the court appeal that we made over Elsie. My dear sister Diney and her children have been utterly disinherited."[9]

Jesse stared, bewildered. "He can't have done."

With Diney's family, the Shermans, they determined to fight it. Charles had been a hard man to please, but Levina and Jesse could scarcely believe that he would be so cruel as to leave them so cut off, as they certainly could not rely on Arkey's kindness to make sure they were secure in their land.

Uncles Claney and Hiram were the executors, and their duty was to gather all of Charles's assets into the probate estate. Levina and the Shermans questioned whether the old man was in sound mind when the will was drawn.

The year before the old man died, Arkey had called upon a neighbor, William E. Kennedy, the circuit court judge for Maury County, and brought him to see Charles. The man was failing and had decided to dictate his will, and he had heard that Judge Kennedy could draw up a proper document for him. With the judge seated in a chair by the table, Charles sat up in his bed in the back of his house, holding a crumpled paper on which he had scribbled his notes. He drank freely of apple cider as he laid out his wishes for the judge. Arkey hovered in the front room, a call away, to remember names that Charles, in his age and in his drink, could not recall or keep straight. Later the judge would swear that Charles was of sound mind and understood what he was doing.[10]

Jesse understood then that they could not continue to stay in Maury County. Soon, he and William left down the Cumberland River to find a place to resettle, which brought them sometime later to Little Rock. They were able to establish themselves relatively quickly there as men of some learning and resourcefulness.[11]

Their brother, Noah, had stayed behind with their mother to continue things until they could follow, hopefully with more assets won from the ongoing lawsuits over Elsie and the will. Noah was to account for their absence when necessary, so as Jesse and William stood in the *Arkansas Gazette* office, Noah might well be in a Columbia courtroom miles away, requesting a delay to one proceeding or another—whether in regard to the will, the Dick, Booker, and Company lawsuit, or one of the other debts.

"Brother, join us."

Jesse turned from the window and walked into Woodruff's office to find that, during his reverie, the others had left William alone with their host, who began talking before Jesse could say a word.

"Gentlemen, I am pleased to become better acquainted with you today. You have done a good turn for Colonel Ashley and the democracy. I understand you are here from Tennessee. Ten years ago, I was in Tennessee myself. I bought my printing press—the one downstairs—in Franklin. I wanted to visit the general while I was there, but I did not get the chance." Woodruff was a Jackson man, and his newspaper provided strong support for the U.S. Administration.

"Did you read the president's message?" Woodruff asked.

Jesse nodded. The *Gazette* had devoted almost two and a half pages of the January 5 issue, printing the entire annual State of the Union address, and, of course, Jesse had studied it at length.

Woodruff continued, "He wrote so eloquently on the wisdom of moving the aborigines to the west of us, outside the pale of our civilization. We can now secure the blessings of liberty and religion in our own country with our own institutions, and they can freely practice their ways in their territory. And their movement through Arkansas will put federal money in our pockets from the ration contracts."

Woodruff paused and looked expectantly from one brother to the other.

"Yes, it was a well-written address," William replied. "We both read it more than once."

"It was discussed at length at the debate society," added Jesse, referencing the essential social group in Little Rock that had, for the past eight years, established regular meetings to discuss the day's important questions. They often met privately for members and sometimes hosted open speeches, debates, or roundtables for the general public. Jesse had yet to become a member, but he had attended several public speeches and expressed interest in the private meetings' discussions. Inwardly, he thought he would need more practice before lending his voice to the group.

"Of course," Woodruff nodded. "I have been in irregular attendance. What is the coming question?"

"Whether wealth has a greater influence on mankind or fame," answered Jesse.

"Fame or wealth?" Woodruff mused. He put on a visage of hard calculation. "It must be fame. Wealth is harder to obtain, so fewer men have it, thereby decreasing its effect over fame." With that, he abruptly rose, straightened his waistcoat, and announced, "Now the press of business is upon me, gentlemen, and I must take your leave."

The brothers nodded and rose to shake the editor's hand as they departed. Shoulder to shoulder, they headed west on the wet street.

"Time for The Eagle?" asked William.

"Yes, I think so. It is a little early for supper, but this business has made me hungry." The only real hotel in town, The Eagle boasted common areas on the first floor, simple rooms on the second floor for passers-through, and a third floor reserved for bachelors who were long-term residents. It had a modest kitchen and bar, making it a place to hear and discuss news from all over.

William looked at Jesse from the side of his eye as they crossed the road, their boots squelching in the mud. "That newspaperman expected you to talk about the government contracts. He was either hoping that you were a puppy who would talk indiscreetly ..."

"... or he was looking for a tell," Jesse finished.

"What does he know, brother?"

"I could not tell."

"Did we reveal anything?"

"I think not."

"Does it matter now, either way?"

Jesse took a deep breath and said, "Probably not."

PART II

4

THE CHOCTAW NATION

The bare cabin's meager fire seemed to cower from the cold outside, hiding its face from such a wicked enemy. As the flames retreated into the glow of the cracked logs, Jesse was relieved to have spent the night indoors. He had never known such a harsh winter. Snow had been scarce in Tennessee, but here, the land outside went beyond snow-laden. Here, brittle ice covered the entirety of nature. Its weight made branches crack and fall in crashes through the night. Mimicking the sound of rifle shots, the breaking boughs kept him awake and on edge. The woods to the north seemed to groan with the cold. To the south, a loose clump of wooden buildings glimmered faintly, marking Washington in the Arkansas Territory.

Jesse sensed the coming dawn and rose to meet it. His muscles were stiff from lying on the puncheon floor, and he ached with the cold. He kicked his legs and shook them, one at a time, to loosen the muscles and get his blood moving.

Conserving the wood as best as he could, he tended to the fire, cursing that so much of what had been gathered the day before remained too wet to burn. The others who shared his shelter shifted on their straw mats, and he moved gently so as not to disturb them.

Casting his eyes toward the lightening sky, he nested the coffee pot in some coals and left the little bare room. He did not really expect to see any change to the east—surely they would not arrive at dawn when they finally did—but glancing toward the east had become an increasingly frequent habit in these weeks of waiting.

He started his morning tasks, checking first the barn where the townspeople sheltered their horses from the harsh weather and then the corral where the cattle were kept. Each morning, one or more might lay dead, and they had to be attended to quickly so the meat was not wasted. The beef was central to his responsibility as he prepared for the coming Choctaw on their emigration from Mississippi.[1]

Throughout the spring and summer of 1831, Jesse had traveled the roads of western Arkansas, often as they were being built. The United States Army Corps of Engineers had extended a road through Washington to Fort Towson, which had been built in 1824 as a military outpost. The fort sat alongside Gates Creek in the Indian Territory and was constructed after the Treaty of Doak's Stand between the United States and the Choctaw Nation. In this treaty, the Choctaw traded land east of the Mississippi River for land west of the Mississippi in the Indian Territory. After the Treaty of Dancing Rabbit Creek, the army built this road to facilitate travel northwest from Washington in the Arkansas Territory to Harris Mills just over the line in the Indian Territory. The road then ran about due west to the fort.[2]

Jesse grew to know this road well, traveling for the sake of the traders in Little Rock and making business connections. Along it, he found a nice piece of unattended land on the Clear Creek prairie. He thought it would make a fine settlement with strategic access to Fort Towson Road to the west. Though he had no legal claim to the land, he and other settlers in the area shared a hope that, when the dust had settled, due consideration would be given to those who had worked and tamed the land, so he began to build some simple shelters. Jesse could see himself established there for a long time, building something in his own name. From there, he could trade with the Choctaw, the soldiers of the fort, and the surrounding farmers. He frequently trekked back and forth from Little Rock to Clear Creek, becoming well-known in the area and building business relationships with the local farmers and traders.[3]

On his July 1831 return to Little Rock, Jesse joined his brother William for a meal, and they found the hotel busier than usual. The federal government had officially requested bids on contracts to supply food to the emigrating Choctaw. For the last few months, the request had been anticipated and discussed among the businessmen of Little Rock and the farmers of Arkansas. That month, news arrived confirming the opportunity.

It had been just what Jesse was waiting for. He and his monied partners had been quietly preparing for weeks. Jesse's deal allowed him an interest in contracts in exchange for seeing them executed. He would find the goods needed by the government, buy them, and see to it that they were delivered on time and to the right place. Their preparations had put them in a good position to bid, and Jesse and his partners won many of the contracts.[4]

Over the next few months and into winter's onset, Jesse and others arranged for the shipment of the necessary goods to arrive ahead of the Choctaw. He negotiated with the local farmers who, knowing that the government had to buy rations for the Choctaw, had doubled the asking price of beef on the hoof and tripled the cost of corn. Jesse had delivered the news to the farms in western Arkansas that the federal government would ship food all the way from Georgia rather than pay such prices. He had returned with the farmer's acquiescence to lower their asking price to fifty cents a bushel. One great need was cattle, and herds had to be tended and kept on the hoof until slaughter was needed.

The fall of 1831 had been a particularly rainy one, and, try as they might, the United States Army could not keep the Arkansas roads from becoming impassable swamps. Finally, it was decided that the Choctaw would travel by steamboat as far as they could, moving in separate groups to keep order and to avoid short rations. One group bound for Fort Towson traveled by steamer from Vicksburg up the Red River to Fulton, Arkansas. The other group traveled by steamer down the Mississippi River from Memphis up the Arkansas River to Little Rock. They would travel by foot and wagon to Washington.

The sky was painted a brutal slate gray on the late November day when Jesse left his settlement for the little town of Washington. He had hoped to arrive just in time to meet the emigrating Choctaw, but the tribe was nowhere to be found.

Now, it was January. The process had been fraught with delays, and it was growing harder to maintain the herd against the harsh winter.[5]

Jesse made it back to their modest shelter around mid-morning. There was a small table just outside the door, and he lowered himself onto the stool next to it, gingerly flexing his cold-stiff legs and knees and warming his hands with a steaming cup. He watched the dawn come up and wished it would give more than its cold light and meager relief from the frost.

He rubbed his hands together and pulled his fur up further around his ears. He ate a bit of dried venison and stiff cornmeal bread, washing the meal down with a swig of bitter coffee. When morning finally produced enough light to read and write, he brought out a letter he had begun the night before to his brother-in-law, George Washington Sherman. He lived back in Columbia, where Jesse's extended absence was undoubtedly causing problems for both his family and his creditors. Jesse read how he had started before continuing.

> *Washington January 14, 1832*
>
> *Dear Sir,*
>
> *I now draft you a few lines to let you know that I am still in the land of the living and doing well. I write to let you know that I can not get to Tennessee as soon as I thought. I will be some twenty or thirty days yet before I can set out for Tennessee owing to the late coming of the Indians. We have just arrived at this place and will set out on tomorrow and will get through in twenty days and I shall come immediately for Tennessee...*

Jesse paused before continuing. He wondered if thirty days was giving himself enough time. It would have to do. He continued his letter.

> *I have made a settlement 80 miles above this place on Red River near the Choctaw line and have got all my buildings nearly done where I intend to live for some years. I have a good stock of goods and sell fast to the white and Indians both. I have five hundred head of cattle...for supplying the Indians which keeps me busy day and night to attend to them.*

His hand cramped from the cold, and he tucked it into his sleeve to warm. The sun had not climbed much more while he sat on this stool, and none of his traveling companions had stirred. After the Choctaw arrived at the fort, Jesse planned to return to Columbia, Tennessee, to use the gains from this difficult post to settle his most pressing debts. He was sure that his family members remaining in Maury County were being hounded about his whereabouts and plans, and since he would be at least another month yet, he hoped he could send along some news that would mollify them for the time being. Flexing his fingers, he returned to his letter.

> *I have an interest in a great many contracts at this time so that it is impossible for me to come at this time. Tell mother that if she has not highered [sic] the Negroes not to higher them for I shall want them very much, She can higher them by the month until I come and to make ready to move with me to this Territory if she intends to come with me. I will soon have my house done and a good [barn] for this country and everything to live on. When I come and I will bring a good lot of money with me. Some of my business I intend to settle up when I come and this time if they will have patience, they will all get paid. I shall not write more at the present as I shall soon come on myself. I am yours with respect.*
> *—J.B. Badgett*

When the Choctaw finally arrived, it was clear that Jesse's trials against the winter had been nothing in the face of their suffering.

The Choctaw were in all manner of dress, many with bare feet and heads, many holding children to their chest, and all shivering in the bitter wind. They had replenished some of their supplies in Little Rock, but it was not enough to prevent so much suffering, as most of the clothes and furs and tents had been sent on to Fort Smith under a previous, discarded movement plan. Jesse had at least his clothes and fur, and, in his role as a contractor, he spent most days on horseback or indoors.

The leader of these Choctaw was Colonel David Folsom, who Jesse found quite impressive. Broad-shouldered and barrel-chested, his dark hair surrounded a face that had gone gaunt in the difficulties of their emigration. His father had been a white settler who married into the tribe. It was clear to Jesse that he was well-respected among the Choctaw, as they followed his instructions without question. Folsom inspected the remaining cattle and other goods Jesse had kept in preparation for their arrival and made a clear and detailed inventory, planning their use and distribution.

For a couple of days, the group rested in the area surrounding Washington while Folsom and Jesse enacted the colonel's plan for the goods: they loaded what would be carried on the wagons and arranged for the herding, slaughter, and preservation of the remaining beef.

As they pushed on towards Fort Towson, Jesse traveled with them to fulfill the final leg of the contract. The following month would be the most brutal of his life. He thought often of how, on the road from North Carolina to Tennessee, he had been struck by his little sister's plaintive cries. Her cries of discomfort were nothing compared to those heard on the trail with the Choctaw. There was pitiful little shelter against the cruel chill. Sickness and pain plagued them, especially the elderly and the young. They had no choice but to push forward, but their progress was limited by the pace of the walking sick.

When they stopped for rest, Jesse conversed with Colonel Folsom, who he found to be an eloquent man of God. He was embittered about the plight of his tribe, but he was also a highly practical man, accepting his fate and facing the future in order to lead them in what freedom and prosperity they could find after this horrid ordeal.

"There is no other course for us," he said often, as much to himself as to whoever was there to hear him. "We must turn our face toward the setting sun and our new homes."

Jesse told him of his settlement and expressed his hope that, when the Choctaw were settled, he could provide for their needs through trades as they established their new homes. Folsom listened, apparently skeptical of Jesse's proposal. Disquieted, Jesse asked him politely about his plans for their establishment in their new lands.

Folsom was quiet for a time. When he finally spoke, his deep voice kept a careful, practiced cadence.

"It will take some years to recover from the losses of this passage," he told him.

Jesse became freshly aware then of the sounds of the encampment, which, over the past few days, had become a background hum of misery. The tribe's healthy spoke little when they rested, saving their strength to care for the sick and lame and injured so they could help them when it came time to move again. But the injured groaned, the children cried weakly in exhaustion, and the sick coughed and spat and heaved with nothing in their bellies to lose. Jesse closed his eyes and tried to focus on Folsom's steady voice as he spoke of their strength as a tribe. Quoting eloquently from the Bible, which he had learned from Presbyterian missionaries and his father Nathaniel, he spoke of Job.[6]

Finally, he remarked on their future as a people, promising them a country that treasured their values. He hoped that, one day, there might be a Constitution of the Choctaw Nation, enshrining his promises to law.[7]

5

THE LITTLE ROCK DEBATING SOCIETY

J esse leaned over the railing of the *Reindeer's* upper deck, watching the banks of the Arkansas River slide by. The great, dark plume from the steamer's smokestack cast a shadow on the turbulent water, giving the impression that a great serpent glided just below the surface. Jesse was on his way back to Little Rock after a buying trip in New Orleans. The Summer of 1832 was hot, and Jesse appreciated the cooling breeze on the deck as he looked out over the western bank, reflecting on his brief dream of settling on the Clear Creek prairie. With no title to the land, Jesse had given up on that plan and lost most of his investment.

Jesse had exaggerated in his letter to George, hoping that the promises he wrote before setting off with the Choctaw would keep his creditors from breathing too heavily down his brother-in-law's neck. While he suspected they would be quite interested in his whereabouts and plans, Jesse had stretched the truth for another reason, too: he hoped that he could make something solid out of the connections he had built during the government's removal of the Choctaw.

It was an admittedly desperate hope.

The cattle he had described in the letter were not truly his, but they did represent a commission for him under government contracts to supply the emigrating tribe. The hope that had gotten him through the bitter winter was dashed well before the March thaw, but Jesse could not wallow in disappointment. He could only look forward to the next bit of road.

After using some of the government contract money to pay off a few scattered debts, Jesse returned to Little Rock. There, he used a large part of the remaining money to fund a new business partnership with his brother William. In December of 1832, they opened the Wm. Badgett & Company storefront, using their experience as store clerks to open a dry goods and grocery business. William was more than happy to have Jesse back from the Indian Territory, and Jesse gladly went to work in their new business. The following year, Jesse was often on the move, buying and selling while William ran the store in Little Rock.[1]

Jesse grew familiar with the route between Little Rock and New Orleans, carrying back produce and cheese and flour to restock the store. When he could find good prices on leather and tinware, he brought those as well, and, if they sold well, the Badgett brothers would add them to their regular order, expanding their inventory and establishing a steady return of custom from Little Rock and the surrounding farms.

Brother Samuel also settled nearby with his wife, Elizabeth. Preferring a quiet life, he remained on the outer edges of Little Rock's energetic buzz and focused on tending his patch of land. Also settling near Little Rock, Jesse's brother Noah had come to live permanently in the Arkansas Territory with his new bride, Lucetta, the step-daughter of his business partner William McLain. Noah would soon be the first of the Badgett brothers to become a family man, as Lucetta was expecting a child. He was more and more a town staple and, with his brothers, was becoming a well-known figure in the area. Jesse hoped that eventually more of their family would come to settle in Little Rock.[2]

His most recent journey back to the capital city was relatively uneventful. Usually, when traveling up from New Orleans, the steamboat would be caught on at least four hidden snags—fallen logs, broken up beaver dams, or drifts of mud from recent flooding—that would completely halt their progress until they could be freed. There had recently been two new boats added to those regularly traveling that stretch, federally-funded steamboats equipped with mechanical cranes. Working in particular sections of the river, the boats were charged with clearing anything shallow enough to hold up regular transportation. While he had been almost disappointed not to catch one of these vessels in action, he marked that their journey seemed smoother than any previous one he had taken, and he arrived back in Little Rock well before expected. Jesse was supervising the unloading of his goods when he heard his name.

"Jesse!" a familiar voice called. "Jesse Badgett!"

Jesse turned and saluted the man coming down the lane towards him. The man had been trotting to catch him but slowed as he saw Jesse coming up the lane to meet him partway.

"I just came from your place," said his friend, a local man named Johnson with whom he had often shared a meal or drink at the hotel. "Samuel was there, but was just leaving. I think he would have waited, but they did not seem to be expecting you so soon."

Jesse marked the sun. It was early afternoon.

"It was an easier trip than my last to New Orleans; we hit far fewer snags along the river. The snagboat had just been through, I think, and that was a great help," he chimed.

"It seems congratulations are in order! Mrs. Badgett has been delivered of her child."

"Lucy?" Jesse asked, although the answer was obvious. "Today? Are they well?"

His friend patted his shoulder. "Three days ago, I believe, from what Mr. Samuel said. He was there for the first happy meeting of a baby boy, name of John."

Jesse smiled broadly and found himself blinking back a sudden threat of happy tears. "The first Badgett born west of the Mississippi," he considered. "Thank you for this news."

His friend patted his shoulder again and turned to be on his way.

"I may have stolen the pleasure of sharing it from one of your brothers in this lucky passing, but I was certainly happy to deliver it. These times, sharing good news is a treat."

His friend strode back toward the center of town. Jesse turned to watch the stevedores and the carters unloading the new goods for the store. He felt light and hopeful.

From its founding, Wm. Badgett & Company grew at a good clip, keeping pace with two other stores that opened in Little Rock's expanding market. Jesse went several times by steamboat to New Orleans, but also to Memphis by horseback and by wagon once the highway was safely established. The Badgett brothers, with vested personal and business interest in travel between Tennessee and Little Rock, added their names to a dozen others from Pulaski County, petitioning the federal government to prevent unlawful detours and toll booths on the road. By the following November, the brothers were also agents for booking passage on the *Arkansas,* a steamboat that routinely carried goods and passengers from Little Rock and New Orleans, stopping at the major landings along the way.[3]

By June of 1834, the brothers moved their wares into a large, two-story building directly across from the Jeffries Hotel. It was a fine store, showcasing a broad range of products. On the left of the first floor, they displayed the groceries and common needs: flour, sugar, coffee, tobacco, soap, and, sometimes, casks of fine bacon. To the right were the dry goods and hardware, such as rolled fabrics and tin pots. On the left side of the second floor, they displayed ladies' and gentlemen's clothing, shoes, and hats. To the right, fine saddlery and leather goods hung on hooks. A small office took up the back corner of the second floor.[4]

As their economic foothold became more secure, so also did their roles in the town's political life. With the support of their friends, William was elected Clerk of the Pulaski County Circuit Court in August of 1833. Later that same year, Jesse was appointed as Territorial Magistrate, and Noah was elected to the town council. Bachelors Jesse and William shared a room at the Jeffries and frequently attended dinners and receptions held in its main room for local accomplishments and distinguished passers-through.[5]

One such dinner honored Captain Jacob Brown, the federal man in charge of provisioning the late emigration of the Choctaw. They spoke quietly in recollection of the Choctaw's horrid experience, Brown explaining some of the causes of confusion that Jesse had not fully understood at the time—political rivalry, the appointment of men who hated each other in positions that required communication and cooperation, and viciously corrupt men who lied to the Choctaw at every opportunity. At the dinner, Jesse gave a short toast in Brown's name, thanking him for his leadership and his continued role in securing the lands west of the Mississippi.[6]

The Little Rock Debating Society also grew, and, with Jesse's help, they pooled their texts and resources to open a public lending library. Jesse's skill as an orator grew as well, and he often coached other young men. It was with these efforts to improve his public speaking that Jesse first became aware of his unconscious habit of holding his arms behind his back. At first, he sought to correct this habit in order to utilize his hands for emphasis and give direction and structure to his talk. After all, the society's library featured not one but two copies of Gilbert Austin's *Chironomia, or A Treatise on Rhetorical Delivery*, which spoke of the crucial importance of gesture and posture to the great Roman orators.

This proved to be difficult for Jesse, and he frequently found himself distracted by the effort, undermining the intended impression. Finally, he abandoned his attempts to visualize Austin's sphere, squared his shoulders and knees accordingly, and resumed his natural stance for all but a few well-chosen gestures. He adopted this strategy for his part in the debate on the question, "Ought imprisonment for debt be abolished?" He kept his hands held relaxed in his usual position behind his back for the majority of his few minutes of speech until, at his conclusion, he drew out one hand in a fist and lightly hit his hip to emphasize his reiteration of each central point. At the finish, he opened his hand, as if dropping the matter at the feet of his audience.

A colleague in the society noticed this change and applauded it. He told Jesse that the quiet nature of his typical posture reflected a man who only spoke when he had something to say. When he opened his mouth, he drew both ear and eye.

On July 4, 1834, the Little Rock Debating Society held a celebration for the fifty-eighth anniversary of American independence. That evening, the society's president, local attorney and former Tennessean Elijah Robertson Childress, hosted a dinner with formal speeches to honor the United States and its leaders. When it came time for the volunteer toasts, Jesse rose. "Our common country—" he began. As he spoke, his hand emerged from behind his back in a fist, which he pressed to his belly. "She has evinced to the world that the rights of man can be enjoyed and perpetuated by a brace and independent people." He opened his fingers and moved his open hand to press over his heart, before punctuating his sentiment with his raised glass.[7]

Only six weeks after the Fourth of July celebration, Jesse sat at the little desk in the back of Wm. Badgett & Company's second floor, reviewing a ledger of passengers that had arrived on the *Arkansas* the day before. A knock on his door drew him away from the paperwork, and he turned to find his brother Samuel standing in the doorway. His cap was in his hand, and he was crushing it out of shape.

"What is it, Sammy?" Though Samuel was a grown man of twenty-one, Jesse sometimes forgot himself and addressed him as he would a baby brother.

"I wish that you would not call me that. Noah sent me," Samuel said and looked around the small office, though it was clear Jesse was alone. "Where's William?" It seemed whatever it was, Samuel did not want to say it twice.

"Is he not downstairs?" Jesse asked. He was about to call for his brother when William appeared at the top of the stairs.

"I am here—I was around back, and I did not see you come in but only heard your voice." William noted Samuel's cap, which was now clasped between his hands, nearly wrung like a dirty rag.

"Noah sent me," Samuel repeated. "His son, John, passed during the night."[8]

William and Jesse looked at each other alarmed, and it was clear that they were both thinking the same thing. They had seen the boy —a bright-eyed two-year-old—only four or five days ago. His color then had been good, with no signs of fever or illness. Jesse remembered how the boy had taken Noah's hat off his head with a single flourish, and William remarked how strong he was getting.

"How can that be?" Jesse asked.

"It came on quickly, so Noah said. The other day he was coughing and wanted water all the time to soothe his throat. Then yesterday he began to refuse all water and took no food. Noah sent for the doctor, but he came too late. The boy's throat had gone all white and clogged, and he succumbed to the infection. Noah is—" Samuel swallowed visibly, and Jesse felt, for a moment, a sympathetic constriction in his own throat. "Noah is quite distraught, as of course is Lucy. They beg off visitors for today, but wanted me to bring you the news."

"Poor little John," William murmured. His brothers gave *hmms* of agreement, and they were quiet for a while as each thought a silent prayer.

6

GONE TO TEXAS

Over a year later in April of 1835, Jesse and William were again in the little back-corner office of their store. It looked quite different—emptier. The saddlery that had lined one wall was gone as well as the stock of folded clothing and bolts of fabric. All had been sold, even the tables that had served as displays for the various goods they had managed to keep in stock for years. Other than a lonely broom propped in one corner, all that remained was the little desk covered from edge to edge in papers and ledgers as William sorted through their records.

The business had begun to struggle in the later months of 1834, and soon they found themselves owing more than they could cover. They had previously managed to stay afloat and recover for a few months by clearing their store in a large cash-only discount sale. However, while the initial event provided enough remainder to restock some essentials, the strategy was proving insufficient a second time. William sat at the desk while Jesse leaned against the wall. Their postures emphasized the difference in their statures—where Jesse was broad-shouldered and muscular, William was long and lean.

William selected a credit slip and squinted at it.

"Five dollars from Mr. Stevens—which one is he?" he asked Jesse.

"The old Englishman. His place is south of Noah's. The one whose beard does not match his pate."

"Ah, yes. Well?"

"Doubtful. He lost two slaves to illness this winter."

William groaned and set the slip aside, adding it to a growing stack. He rubbed at his face with both hands. They had been at the task for some time and it was wearying, not because it was strenuous, but because it was disheartening. In the pile of credit slips, they searched for debtors to call on—those to whom they could apply some pressure for collection, allowing them to pay their own debts. They owed over four thousand dollars, all told, including real estate mortgages.

"Truth is," William said, "we need them all."[1]

Jesse nodded thoughtfully and took a pen to a scrap of paper. He hunched over the desk and wrote a short paragraph before passing it to William to consider. William nodded, but also picked up the pen, scratching out phrases and substituting others. He handed it back to Jesse who added a few lines. In silence, they did this back and forth for a few more turns before, finally, William nodded his final approval.

"Will you copy it out plain and take it? I'll pack the rest of this up and meet you at The Jeffries."

Jesse nodded and set to work copying the notice to be printed in the *Arkansas Times and Advocate*:

The subscriber having disposed of the entire stock of Dry Goods belonging to the firm of Wm. Badgett & Co. earnestly desires all persons indebted to said firm, to come forward and settle their accounts either by note or otherwise, as the business of the firm is about to be closed, and they wish to square the books. All who cannot pay up at present will be required to give their notes.

He tenders his acknowledgments to the citizens of the surrounding country, for the very liberal patronage they have received since their establishment in business in this place and he hopes that all who have been favored with a credit, will not be backward in complying with this call.

He has taken a room in the white building connected with the Mr. Jeffries' hotel, where he or his brother can at all times be found to attend to business connected with the firm.

Wm. Badgett

Little Rock, April 10, 1835.[2]

And so it was that the Badgetts set about closing the business they had opened just a little over two years prior. Over the next several months, they collected the debts and notes their notice had called for, relinquishing the two-story building to another merchant.

To his discontent, Jesse also found that the Little Rock Debating Society was losing momentum and the interest of the town. The town's men of Little Rock now favored the immediate questions of the present moment over the abstract questions of society. As more people moved to the Arkansas Territory, the push was on for statehood, and Arkansans speculated how life would change once they added their star to the United States flag. A census had confirmed they had the necessary population, and there was near constant consideration of whether this change would come before the next year's election and who would be retained from the current councils in the formation of the new state government.[3]

One Friday afternoon that late fall, Jesse and William joined a dozen other men who had gathered in the big room at The Jeffries to discuss the question of a cannon buried in Texas. The brothers were impressed at the noise of the gathering. Men stood in groups to discuss the latest official and unofficial updates. It had been a month since the fight at Gonzales, a skirmish between the North American settlers and the Mexican Army over the weapon. In the days since, as more news of and reactions to the incident circulated, the weight of the matter grew.

"The Battle of Gonzales. They're calling it the Lexington of Texas," one man said.[4]

Jesse and William moved through the room, taking in the talk.

The long-term residents of The Jeffries had a custom of pooling the money needed for regular delivery of the newspapers, a half dozen copies to be shared. The brothers could see by the way the men were scattered about that Friday's edition had not yet been delivered. The talk was just rumor and conjecture, no more than a frenzied rehashing of what they had been hearing for weeks.

A pair of men stood by the bar with their arms crossed, talking idly.

"It was lucky for the Texians that Davis had just sent his plow through his peach orchard," one man mused. "They were able to bury it while the others delayed the Mexicans until the reinforcements had come."

"Weren't lucky for them that dog barked that night in the fog and gave away their hiding place, though," the other responded.

Jesse and William exchanged a look and stood apart from the general crowd. While the events had fascinated the brothers, they preferred to wait for the dispatch of more news rather than engage in idle speculation about old reports.

Mexico had gained independence from Spain in 1821, but for many years suffered under a succession of short-lived governments. General Antonio Lopez de Santa Anna was often a leader in these various governments. As president in 1835, he abrogated the popularly-adopted Constitution of 1824, an act that led to armed rebellion in several Mexican states. Rumors of the growing discontent had circulated for many months, but not so long before—only the previous September—the *Arkansas Times* reported that the rumors were unfounded, reprinting a letter from Sam Houston himself that denied the need to gather a militia. Houston described Texas as tranquil, but how quickly that had changed after October's first shots of rebellion.

The brothers had heard how, fearful of losing their independent ability to protect their town, the men of Gonzales had refused to turn over their only weapon of note—a mounted bronze six-pounder cannon. They temporized the Mexican authorities, delaying them some days by secreting away the ferry that crossed the river and hiding the cannon by burying it in the loose soil until reinforcements could join them. With each day, the news and rumors seemed to carry new degrees of insult from the Mexican government: in one story, the officers had ordered an encampment on a settler's farm and then made free with his watermelons. Conversely, each passing day seemed to highlight the settlers' ingenuity against the Mexican Army's unfair demands. The people of Gonzales had even prepared shots for the cannon by cutting up pieces of chains and forging iron balls out of scrap.

The settlers were determined. And war seemed inevitable.

Jesse and William had discussed it between themselves each evening, the implications blooming in their minds.

The door to The Jeffries swung open, and a boy entered carrying two stacks of newsprint; one was the hotel's subscription. The other, the boy began to sell to the men standing around. Jesse took their copy from the prior-purchased stack, and William followed him to a nearby table.

Before Jesse could have a proper look, William asked, "What news from Texas?"

"Hold, I am looking," Jesse said, putting him off. "Here." He brought the section closer to read aloud.

Important from Texas.

There is a report just come which I rely on, that the Mexicans at Gonzales have been defeated, and forty killed besides wounded; no loss on our side; the fight was in the woods. The enemy had cavalry. All goes on well. Upwards of one hundred leave here to-day, some from Trinity; fifty will go on to-morrow. I think there will be 800 on the frontier in a week. The enthusiasm increases daily; there are no peace-men, on parties here now—all are war men. I have remained here because it was thought that I would be of more service to unite opinions and hurry out men. I shall go to the frontier soon. The enemy must cross the Nueces before the campaign ends. We will then organize a government for Texas. I recommend dispatch in sending to the United States. Let them know how matters stand, and that the country is united and firm, and therefore invincible.

Yours respectfully,
S. F. Austin[5]

"800—" William breathed.

Jesse looked at his brother and saw that his eyes were lit by the idea. They had discussed already whether they would answer a call to arms and join those in Texas. They had settled as much of their debts as they could and still owed a great deal—more than they could pay in dribs and drabs. Their territorial political offices would soon be ended, and with them, their salaries. As Arkansas was moving towards statehood, William had not run for re-election.

They were in need of something to change their fortunes. A newly-freed Texas would present opportunities for those who had fought to free her. Jesse could see that this latest news from Austin, added to all they had heard and read for the past month, had been enough to settle William's mind.

Still, he was not so sure.

He had heard the talk of the men leaving for the frontier with freshly purchased rifles, ready to "stain with hostile blood their maiden arms." Jesse did not fear combat, but he was not violent by nature and was more hesitant to go seeking it out.

William looked around the room a moment.

"I don't see Charles," he said, scanning the room for their acquaintance, Charles Rice, former editor of the *Arkansas Times and Advocate*. He often had more context to add to what was printed and a clear eye for discerning facts from rumors.

As Jesse returned to the newspaper, William rose from the table. "I'm going to find him and speak to him about this news. Shall I bring him back here?" Jesse nodded, and William departed.

Jesse continued along the same column. News of the stirrings in Texas had reached the east coast. As Jesse read on, his eyes went naturally to the phrase "*—and a hint is thrown out that there will be Declaration of Independence.*" Here, Jesse felt the same stirring that he saw in his brother. While he was not eager to fight, he had to wonder what it would be like to see such a thing as a revolution, to be there when men decided for themselves how they would be governed. *"So did their forefathers in the United States. The same blood—the same love of liberty lives in their veins, and they must and will be free in spite of Santa Ana."*

Jesse looked up from the paper, but William had not yet returned with Charles. Jesse turned the page and continued to scan for more news from Texas. He did land on another mention of Texas, but it was not in regard to revolution.

> *We learn from the* New Orleans Bee *that it is in contemplation in that city to connect New Orleans with the Gulf of California on the Pacific by a rail road to run through Texas, via Nacogdoches and the gorge of the Rocky Mountains. It is computed that by extending the contemplated rail road from New Orleans to Natchez and thence to Richmond, there would be a continuous rail road of 1600 miles from New Orleans to New York, which would be traveled in four days! Should the Rail road to California be effected, steam ships would communicate from the latter to China, Persia or the East and thus not only cut up the East India Shipping of the Northern States, but render the projected route across the Isthmus of Panama unnecessary.*

Jesse marveled at the idea. He had never traveled by rail and imagined what such a journey would be like, covering the whole of the country from north to south in a matter of days before continuing west through the wide-open country until the mountains rose from the horizon. He was lost in reverie when William and Charles joined him at the table, along with Nathaniel Dennis. Jesse knew that Charles had considered joining the volunteers on behalf of Texas, and he suspected that, since Nathaniel was joining them at the table, he was also considering it. Or, perhaps, he had already decided and was looking for traveling companions. Jesse contemplated his brother, who wore a solemn expression that could not hide his excitement. William, it seemed, was decided, too.

On November 20, the *Arkansas Times* would feature the historic

call to arms sent by General Houston himself, which began as
follows:

> Department Orders:
>> Head Quarters Texas
>> Department of Nacogdoches, Oct. 8 1835
>> The time has arrived when the revolutions of the interior of Mexico
>> have resulted in the creation of a Dictator, and Texas is compelled to
>> assume an attitude defensive of her rights, and the lives, and property of
>> her citizens. Our oaths and pledges to the constitution have been preserved
>> inviolate. Our hopes of promised benefits have been deferred. Our constitu-
>> tions have been declared at an end, while all that is sacred is menaced by
>> arbitrary power! The priesthood and the army are to mete out the measure
>> of our wretchedness. War is our only alternative! WAR IN DEFENSE OF
>> OUR RIGHTS MUST BE OUR MOTTO.[6]

However, Jesse and William would not read the announcement
around a table at The Jeffries, for by that time, they had already
resolved to enlist in the Volunteer Army of Texas. They had discussed
ways and means for only an hour or so before it was decided that
night at the hotel. Jesse, William, Charles, and Nathaniel headed
down the Southwest Trail by horseback the very next morning. Once
again, Jesse found himself on the road with the rising sun to his
back.[7]

7

THE SINGULAR LETTER

The Southwest Trail took the four men from Little Rock to the Red River port of Fulton, Arkansas, where they boarded a steamboat for the trip downriver to Natchitoches, Louisiana. They bought horses when they disembarked. There were plenty of mustangs for sale, a breed favored by Tejanos as best suited to their needs and the terrain. Although he considered the mustangs, Jesse instead paid a premium for a chestnut Morgan—a larger, stronger horse that was rare on the frontier and better suited for her intended service in a revolutionary army. As Jesse grew to know the mare, he found her spirited and talkative, prone to voice her thoughts in whinnies and neighs. The horse was beautiful with her tall stature and clean mane. With growing affection for the mount, he named her Athena.

From Natchitoches, they followed the Old San Antonio Road through San Augustine to Nacogdoches and into Mexican Texas, which they found crowded with other hopeful revolutionaries, newly arrived from the United States.

All about Nacogdoches was an excited tension that underscored the urgency of a place on the cusp of war.

The small town harbored many intrigues with various goals and dreams. Seeing opportunity in chaos, supporters of failed filibusters tried to revive their schemes, and grifting land speculators sought buyers among the naive newcomers. Military commanders recruited both veterans and men whose experience of war was limited to fireside stories and historical novels; men whose ambitions were so untethered to reality that they sometimes appeared to suffer from a disease of the mind.

Rumors abounded. Unconfirmed reports raised various alarms about the approach of Santa Anna and the Mexican Army and about the cruelty of their actual and intended actions. Winding up the volunteers, paranoia became part of the atmosphere. So much was unknown that each passing day built excitement and dread in equal measure. Every bit of news came beset with questions and doubts.

Nevertheless, the majority of the volunteers were upbeat, spurred by the spirit of their own independence, a burning desire to fight in desperate battle, and their hope of securing a nice, large piece of bounty land in exchange for their military service. It did not take the Arkansans long to conclude that many of these men were without the means to pay for food, shelter, and further transportation. A surprising number of them did not have the necessary implements of war or the money to buy them.[1]

Fortunately for the Badgett brothers, money was not a problem, as they held on to the proceeds from their store's liquidation.

Using letters of introduction from notable friends in Little Rock, they met with some prominent men in Nacogdoches. Before committing themselves, they split up to observe, meeting again toward the end of the day to discuss what they had learned over a meal. They had no military experience, but they had their own informed abilities to strike up a conversation and discern a few facts from the hopes and rumors of the day.[2]

On November 15, 1835, Jesse and his comrades enlisted in the loosely organized Volunteer Army of Texas, an official entity established by the Provisional Government of Texas. They were soon headed farther south along the Old San Antonio Road to join the Siege of San Antonio de Bexar, a town held by regular Mexican Army units commanded by General Martin Perfecto de Cos. Along the road, they learned that the Texians had defeated General Cos, who surrendered and agreed to march his men out of Texas.[3]

By the time they reached San Antonio, the victorious Texian force of about six hundred had dwindled by more than half as the colonist-soldiers went home to celebrate and to tend to the welfare of their families. The remaining men were mostly recent arrivals from the United States who spoke with great pride of the Siege and their defeat of Cos. A lieutenant of artillery, William Ridgeway Carey showed Jesse the hole in his hat made by a bullet that had grazed his skull but left him gratefully standing and otherwise unhurt. With iron will and good luck, they had taken the place, but now the soldiers were idle and restless, their commanders divided on what to do next.

The town was physically unlike any other place that Jesse had seen. He was used to settlements comprised of newly constructed homes, built quickly of wood to be put to use immediately if needed for practical purposes. New Orleans had some impressive row houses and churches, but the stone and adobe buildings of San Antonio seemed to Jesse's eyes to be ancient, like something from a book.

The town was divided from the fort by a small creek that emanated from a spring. The fort, known locally as the Alamo after the Spanish name for the poplar trees that grew nearby, was a complex of stone-walled buildings and enclosures—the remains of the Mission San Antonio de Valero. Originally intended by Spanish Catholic Franciscans as a religious outpost from which to spread their faith, it was never finished. The church had been deconsecrated and the buildings had been used for various secular functions, including as a shelter against attacks by the Comanche. General Cos had converted and adapted the complex for use as a fort during the Siege of Bexar.

The new arrivals soon learned that Dr. James Grant and Colonel Francis White Johnson wanted the remaining men to join them in an expedition to cross the Rio Grande and capture Matamoros, a wealthy inland port city off the Gulf of Mexico. They counted on support from a population ready to depose Santa Anna and restore the Federal Constitution of the United Mexican States of 1824.

Indeed, no soldier could escape the arguments of Grant. The man roamed about and spoke fervently to them about his plans, boasting that he knew more of the war than any military general. Due to his superior intelligence and university education, he believed he could lead them to capture the riches of Matamoros.

Jesse listened without comment but found Grant's plans inadequate. It was true that Matamoros was a city of thousands, including many Mexicans as well as English and American traders who were disgusted by the cruel, centralist regime that had abandoned the constitution under Santa Anna. But it did not follow logically that the city could be taken by a Texian force of a few hundred or that it would welcome Grant and Johnson and yield itself to their leadership and control.

While Grant addressed a large group of soldiers with his milk-and-honey promises, Jesse felt a tug on his sleeve and gave his ear to the soldier next to him. The man spoke quietly, so as not to be heard by more than those standing immediately near them. "He will not mention it, but Grant just wants his hacienda back."

Jesse raised an eyebrow, not understanding, so the man continued in a low tone. "Grant bought a house and some land near Parras in Coahuila awhile back, but Santa Anna confiscated it along with other foreigner-bought land. I reckon he wants it back." Jesse nodded that he understood but offered no comment.

Grant continued to speak. Jesse heard his words, but his attention was on watching the faces of his fellow soldiers. While there were a few frowns, some giving small shakes of their head over stiff-crossed arms, in most others he saw lit eyes and set jaws. He could see that the doctor's pitch was having the intended effect, stirring the blood of the restless soldiers, but there was something about the hacienda that bothered Jesse like a thorn in his brain.

As he turned to the others, Jesse was not surprised to see that Charles and Nate appeared to be taken in by Grant, but he was disturbed to see that excitement lit William's eyes as well. It was then that the hair on Jesse's neck stood up, and he felt the cold chill of a realization.

"William," he said, pulling his brother a couple steps away from the group. "This man is only interested in himself and his own enrichment and elevation. Does he not remind you of Uncle Arkey?"

"Ha! No, brother, he is nothing like that. He wants to fight for independence and freedom! That's why we're here!"

"No, no, think about what he says. His premises do not lead to his conclusions. He has no military experience. His plans are either vapor or nonsense."

"His premises? Is that a fancy something you picked up in debates?"

Jesse ignored this dig. "Listen closely to him. He has few facts, if any. His logic is faulty. He leaps from a partial truth to a lie. He wants us to accept that only he can capture Matamoros. He has no respect for...well...no respect for anything except himself."

"You just do not like him, Jesse. He is a man of action."

By now, Nate had turned his attention to the brothers' conversation. "What do you know about war, Jesse? Grant was a colonel in the Mexican militia and in the Siege army, too."

"No, just think. You heard Colonel Johnson himself say that our whole number may not be enough to hold this place, yet this place must be held. The Mexican Army will return but must attack us from outside these stone walls. Out there, you are exposed all the way to Matamoros. There is nothing that I can say to them." He gestured to the expedition men who were loading wagons with supplies. "But to you, I say: stay here with me. Do not follow that man. The expedition is doomed. You could be killed."

"He makes sense to me, Jesse," said Nate. "Charles and I are going with him."

"I want to go, too, Jesse," said William.

"William! Do not be a fool, even if they are!" Jesse told him, ever acting as the frustrated older brother. "Stay here with me where it is safer."

Nate bristled and stood up straighter. "Am I a fool? Is this not why we came? To test ourselves in battle? Where is battle to be found in this place? Are you afraid to fight? The Mexicans have gone and Grant says that they will not be back. We must go out to find them. In Matamoros."

Jesse had at some point unconsciously gripped his friend's elbow in his hand. Nate looked at it pointedly, and Jesse let go and took a step back. He would not fight it any further, as it was clear that both of their minds were fixed.

The argument had made up William's mind, and he decided to stay. Accordingly, the brothers had said little more to their friends as the expedition prepared to set off, but each knew that there was no telling when or if they would see each other again. Jesse walked with William down the road until they saw that Nate and Charles had to mount and move on at the pace of the others. A hundred yards down the road, Nate turned in his saddle to look back, and Jesse waved his hat as the disturbed dust billowed up behind his comrades.[4]

As the brothers walked silently back toward town, Jesse's thoughts for his friends were interrupted by another private, who told him to report to his commanding officer, Lieutenant Colonel James Clinton Neill.

With his hands behind his back, Jesse took his leave of William and slowly trudged to headquarters, where Neill cordially offered greetings and a seat. "Jesse, I understand that your friends have gone with Grant."

"Yes sir, we traveled from Little Rock with them. They were burning for a fight. I am worried about them. Grant is headed for trouble."

"That doctor is a reel in a bottle, and his thinking is a puzzle to me. A puzzle with missing pieces. I do not understand him." Neill shook his head bitterly. "But I do understand your concern for your friends. That expedition is a problem, but there is time to find a remedy. Perhaps they will not get far and will return wiser. Here and now, we must hold together what remains. We must do what we can do now to prepare for a return of the Mexican Army."[5]

Jesse frowned and nodded his agreement. It made sense to him that the Mexican Army would return and try to retake San Antonio, which sat at the center of many roads that, if captured, might prove fatal for a free Texas. It was the key to advancing upon the United States colonists.

"Jesse, I have some important business with you. Captain Blair speaks highly of you, and I have read your letters of introduction. You are well regarded by your friends in Little Rock, but they mention no military experience."

Jesse shook his head, "No, sir. This is my first go. We did a little drill in Nacogdoches and I can use a rifle, a musket, and these pistols."

Neill nodded. "I must now take stock of what is left to us and send letters to General Houston and to Governor Smith in San Felipe. Sam will have questions, so a military man should go to the general. For Henry, I need a man with some government experience to put my letter *directly* in his hands." Neill paused to ensure Jesse caught his emphasis. Jesse nodded. "Talk with him if he will talk. I want him to know what I really think about our situation. And I need to know what he really thinks about getting us some help."

Neill paused, then as an afterthought added, "Frank Johnson will be there soon, spinning his tale to the General Council."

He gave Jesse a sort of smile. "The express rider to San Felipe must also be a man who supports our governor and our independence, a good rider who has his own horse and the money to support himself and his animal on the road for ten days, because I can provide no horse or money here."

Jesse thought this task sounded more aligned with his strengths than the alternative of building fortifications at the old church. "Yes, sir. I can do that. I have not been to San Felipe before, but I will go to the governor for you."[6]

"Good." Neill stood, slapping his knees for emphasis.

"Now, we have work to do. I must inspect the fortifications and stores to see what is left. I want you with me for some of that time so that you will know our situation first-hand. Use the rest of the day to make your preparations for the ride. We will start here early tomorrow."

The next day, Jesse reported to Neill. They reviewed the scant paperwork available, took stock of the remaining men and their relevant skills, inspected the decrepit hospital and damaged fortifications, and noted the meager availability of clothing, ammunition, food, horses, equipment, and medical supplies. Jesse was stunned by what they observed and by what it said about their ability to defend the place. Grant and his ill-advised mission had left them nearly naked with such slim rations that the men were mere days away from real hunger. With each passing day, the remaining men grew angrier with Grant for leaving them in this condition.

Especially cruel was the state of the hospital, which had been set up on the second floor of what had originally been intended for use as a friary. The men left there were the sick and wounded from the siege, but Grant's "Federal Volunteer Army," though commanded by a medical doctor, had taken most of the medical supplies needed to care for them.

As Jesse ascended the stone staircase to the ward and entered the crowded space, the sour, coppery stink of blood and infection momentarily overwhelmed him. Taking a quick step back from the room, he expelled breath from his nose violently, an involuntary reaction to the sensory assault. Breathing through his mouth, Jesse forced himself to return.

Men lay on cots that crisscrossed the room with only the narrowest zig-zagging path between them. There was a constant cacophony as they shifted and groaned, trying desperately to find just enough ease to sleep through their pain. Many of the injured lay partly naked or in blood-soaked rags with nothing clean to replace them. Though the winter had been mild so far, the feverish men shivered under thin sheets. As Jesse listened, Neill discussed matters with Dr. Amos Pollard, the chief surgeon of garrison. Later, back at headquarters, the two men sat, and Neill regarded Jesse with grim, gray eyes.

"We are in a dire state." His words were matter-of-fact, but his voice was cold, steely, and tired.

Jesse said nothing, for there was nothing to add to the bare fact.

Neill silently opened a drawer of a great oak desk and removed a pen and a few ink bottles, each lighter than the last. He opened each of the other drawers but found only two pieces of blank writing paper covered with stains and smudges. Neill cursed, then exclaimed with dark humor, "That genius Grant did not leave enough paper for me to write up my reports against him."

Their quick laughter relieved some tension, the moment's lightness a needed break from the foul mood in which their day's work had left them. But the spirit quickly died.

"Jesse," Neill started, haltingly. "Could you advance the cost of paper to support the revolution?"

"Yes, of course, sir. I can do that." Jesse could see the need had somewhat embarrassed his commander, so he left quickly on his errand. After getting directions from an orderly, he procured the needed writing paper. He had to pay the local merchant an exorbitant fee for the scarce sheets, but he quickly returned to Neill's office with his purchase.[7]

That night he was restless, haunted by memories of the suffering Choctaw, thoughts triggered by the agonized soldiers he had seen in the hospital.

In the morning, he reported to Neill, who was busy elsewhere until the afternoon. On his own initiative, he visited every shop and stall in town to buy whatever he could find that might help the sick and wounded. The merchants were eager to sell, preparing for the possibility of having to vacate the area quickly should the violence escalate, but prices were still high. Altogether, he found twenty-four bottles of the local Madera wine for their pain. He bought other supplies as well.

The hospital was up a narrow set of stairs, and Jesse enlisted the help of an enslaved man of about twenty who was returning from hauling water to the barracks; Jesse led the way with one crate, and the man followed with another. As they neared the top, the fort's resident mouser—an orange and white cat that could usually be spotted trotting along the parapets as if on some urgent mission of his own— let out a holler of protest as Jesse, the crate blocking his view of the steps, trod upon his scraggly, bottle-brush tail.

Startled, Jesse nearly toppled backward down the stairs after the fleeing cat, but the enslaved man behind him pushed his crate sharply into Jesse's back, saving them both a hard fall. The jostled bottles of Madera in the crates clanked loudly as Jesse regained his feet and quickly hopped up the remaining two steps.[8]

He turned back down the stairs and spat, "Damn beast!" at the fleeing cat, who disappeared into the dusty yard.

Dr. Pollard came out of the hospital door at a trot to ask after the clamor, looking from Jesse at the top of the stairs to the enslaved man a few steps back.

Jesse shook his head and chuckled. "My apologies for the disturbance, Amos. That darn cat nearly broke my neck." Jesse had not found much levity in the previous weeks and with his feet once more firmly beneath him, he let out a full belly laugh. "Would have, were it not for him," he added, gesturing to the man who had saved him. The enslaved man seemed relieved that it was the cat, not himself, that Jesse had blamed for the near-catastrophe.

"I apologize for Consuelo. He a good mouser. Good with patients, too. But he has a mind of his own," Dr. Pollard said, waving the men over to him.

At that, Jesse nearly laughed again, this time at the ridiculousness of naming a cat. However, seeing that the doctor was serious, he stifled his chortle and followed the man into the hospital to store the materials Jesse had brought.

When they finished, Dr. Pollard dismissed the man to his water-hauling duty, and Jesse commented to the doctor, "There's a fine hand with some sense."

"John is a good man," Dr. Pollard said. Jesse turned to him frowning slightly, hearing in his tone a note of correction and disapproval.

"Is he a freed Black?" Jesse asked. He had not known many freed Africans.

"No," Dr. Pollard answered. "He is still yet in bondage."

Jesse was quiet a moment before continuing. "Excuse my boldness. I am still learning the politics here. I have heard that you are an abolitionist. Is that true?"

"It is my hope that in a free Texas, all men would be free, yes," Dr. Pollard replied, raising his head from his work to give Jesse his eyes, sincere and firm.

Jesse shook his head. "How can a free country be built without industry? How can the land be turned and made profitable without slave hands?"

"There can be industry—cotton, crop, all of it—without slavery," Dr. Pollard said firmly. "There must be."

Jesse wanted to scoff, to ask Dr. Pollard what the professional man knew of the work of growing cotton. To ask of the chaos and violence that would follow from such a path, and for whose good it would be. In the end, however, he could see the resolution in the doctor's face and decided not to debate the issue and risk making an enemy of the man. He simply asked instead, "Are there many in Texas who share your position on the matter?"

"No. Not nearly enough," Dr. Pollard replied. "Not yet."[9]

That night, Jesse remembered the doctor's words. He thought of Elsie and her children and felt uneasy. The doctor's sincerity had struck him, but he could not imagine such a shift. He was a cotton man who had been raised with enslaved workers since infancy. After much tossing and turning, the day's fatigue overtook him, and he found rest. When he woke, he thought no more about it.

Neill first sent official reports to General Houston, his commanding officer. He then completed his reports to Governor Smith, calling Jesse to his office to receive his orders on January 5, 1836.

Neill spoke familiarly to Jesse as he gathered the final drafts, asking questions about Middle Tennessee, where he had also spent some time, asking about this family and that farm. After some time, Neill fell silent, and when he spoke again, his tone had shifted.[10]

"You have seen how Grant left us. Henry must understand the urgency of our plight here. When you deliver these letters, add your voice to mine and make him understand."

"I will, sir."

"And while you are there, look around and let me know what you see and hear."

"Yes, sir."

"Texas will be free and independent, Jesse," Neill said ardently.

"Yes, sir, it will." Jesse nodded solemnly, basking in his revolutionary pride.

He watched as Neill gathered and folded together the pages of his dispatches. The one Neill had just finished writing stood apart from the others since it did not bear the same official signature as the others—*Lt. Col. J. Neill, Commandant of Bexar*—but only the mark of his initials, indicating a direct and personal note rather than an official report for the record. It was this set of pages, folded and sealed, that Neill held out as he wrapped the others in wax-treated canvas and secured them firmly with twine.

"This one is separate, Jesse. Keep it safe. It is only for Henry. Put it in his hands. He should read it first."

Both Athena and the weather favored Jesse on the ride to San Felipe de Austin, capital of the Provisional Government. He had always been fast on a horse and had, over the years, developed an eye for a mare capable of a long, quick journey. Such a horse must take the times of rest as seriously as the going, readily accepting food and water in preparation for the next push. Jesse found himself wishing he had a counting device for the mount's hooves like his father had had for their wagon wheel, for the horse took up the road at what he estimated was over fifty miles a day.

He spent the darkest hours of the first night encamped on the western bank of the San Marcos River. At dawn, he gathered water and ate and smiled to see that Athena was taking his cue, earnestly cropping the grasses by the riverbank. By the time the sun was high enough to see the ford, the mare stood steady at his shoulder, ready to safely make the crossing.

It was two more days and nights before Jesse reached the first cluster of cabins that marked the edge of the town. With the help of a blacksmith who was tending his furnace near the central square, he found the rented building that housed the Provisional Government. He had to wait some time for the governor to be personally available.

Smith greeted him with the practiced and formal warmth of a working politician. His soft brown hair receded back from his temples and his round face was cleanly shaven, giving him an air of authority that seemed at odds with his makeshift surroundings. Along with the package of reports and dispatches was the letter that Jesse pressed upon the governor as a personal note from Neill.

Smith opened it and began to read, and, as he read, his countenance darkened. Jesse did not know exactly what Neill had written, but it was plain that it provoked a great swell of anger in the governor.

After muttering some imprecations and cursing under his breath, Smith composed himself and asked Jesse a few questions about Grant and his plundering for the expedition. He asked, too, about the morale of the remaining garrison. Smith listened to the answers with concerned attention while mechanically unbinding the canvas package to take inventory of its contents and arrange the papers on the simple table that served as a desk.

Smith remained silent while Jesse spoke, growing grimmer and angrier with each response. It seemed this news from Neill had confirmed his worst expectations about the Bexar situation.

"This foolishness will sink us all." Smith muttered something else that Jesse could not quite catch but which may have been *snakes*. Then in a clear voice, he said, "Thank you, Mr. Badgett. Please stay in town until I can send you news to take back to Colonel Neill. There's a room in the back that you may bunk in. There are two others there now, but surely they have risen for the day and you can have a place to rest after you have seen to your horse."

Jesse understood he was dismissed, so he took his leave to stable Athena and get some rest.[11]

The following Sunday afternoon, January 10, 1836, a great deal of rumors spread about the town. The squat building the Council called the town hall was shut up tight in secret session. Jesse visited all the streets and shops, listening to men talk about war and politics so that he might have answers to Neill's questions. It was not until Monday, when the proceedings of the secret meeting were made public, that Jesse learned what the governor had done and how shaky the ground beneath the Provisional Government really was.

Governor Smith was disgusted by Grant's acts and by the intrigues of Colonel Johnson. He believed that those transgressions were aided and abetted by members of the General Council who did not put Texas first. Accordingly, he had peremptorily dismissed the Council and promised to govern alone in the remaining weeks before the Convention met up north in the town of Washington, Texas on March 1.

He allowed Jesse to read his copy of the letter he had addressed to the Council since it would shortly be part of the public record. He minced no words in castigating their individual and collective actions as detrimental to their cause, calling out "Judases in the camp" and men who, "if possible, would deceive their God." He asked those who were still honest to "drive out the wolves," though he refrained from naming the men he saw as "Judases," would-be deceivers, and "wolves." Those accusations were fighting words on the frontier.[12]

"If they admit their errors and reverse the plans of the Matamoros expedition, we may yet be saved from disaster," he told Jesse. "But first they will need to gain an ounce of sense. From whence that will come, I cannot guess."

Jesse gave the governor due deference and thanked him for his candor before again taking his leave.

That evening, Jesse spoke with those council members who would talk, for he doubted that they would bow to the governor's declaration dissolving the Council. Those who would speak shared only what would soon be published and gave him no promise or hint of what plans were on their horizon to support Neill. As they put it to Jesse, the council considered themselves the immediate representatives of the sovereign people, and they would be charging Governor Smith with malfeasance and misconduct. That afternoon, the Council deposed Governor Smith and, in his place, installed Lieutenant Governor James W. Robinson. There was a stalemate when each man refused to work with the other.

The Provisional Government of Texas had essentially ceased to function before Jesse left town.

He had enjoyed the four-day ride to San Felipe, feeling the thrill of his mission and the constancy of his mare. In a matter of days, he had witnessed the government of Texas neutered by political infighting. On the return journey, he felt dread along with a cold, hard tightness in his throat. He had been sent to secure succor and was returning with the news that none could be expected.

Lieutenant Colonel Neill and his command were alone.

8

THE BEXAR RESOLUTIONS

Overwhelmed by the events in San Felipe, Jesse took the days on the trail to ponder what he had seen and heard and frame an intelligent report for Colonel Neill.

When he reached San Antonio on January 16, he quickly noticed that the garrison had left their billets in town and the men were concentrated in the fort. He stabled Athena and walked through the Alamo. It was plain to see that, in his absence of only eleven days, the soldiers had desperately tried to fortify a compound that was ill-suited for the task. Damaged entrenchments dug by the Mexican Army in the Siege of Bexar were now in good repair. Captured cannons had been placed on the walls guarding the approaches. The place looked more like a fort than he remembered.

Jesse found Neill at his new headquarters discussing the work with Major Green Berry Jameson, a man about the same age as Jesse. Jameson was a lawyer and served as the chief engineer superintending the work on fortifications and artillery emplacement.

Neill beckoned for him to enter and offered him a seat and a tin of cooled coffee, which he accepted with thanks. The colonel introduced him to Jameson and told his subordinates that he must end their first meeting to hear what Jesse had to say about San Felipe.

"Major, I slowed my approach when I rode up. The cannon looked ready to fire at me. That will give our men confidence, and other men hesitation," Jesse said, complimenting the major's work.

He smiled and nodded vigorously. "Exactly. We can whip ten to one with our artillery, which I must get back to. Colonel, if there's nothing more, sir, I'll return to my duties."

Neill waited until Jameson was out of earshot before speaking.

"Now, Jesse, what news? What can Henry do for us? Is the Council —" Neill stopped himself after seeing the grim look on Jesse's face, and flatly repeated, "What news?"

Jesse handed over a packet of letters and reported all that he had witnessed in San Felipe. He related much of Smith's letter to the Council from memory and described the impotence of the Provisional Government. He stuck closely to the facts, just as he had in his work as a magistrate, but his impression of the situation in San Felipe was unmistakable.

Neill listened and turned away to watch the dry fire of a gun crew from the window, giving Jesse only his shoulder and face in profile. When Jesse had finished, Neill stood still in this posture for some minutes. Jesse had a sudden empathy for his commanding officer, glad that the responsibility for dealing with the situation was not his.

Finally, Neill said, "What is your impression of the situation back there?"

Jesse hesitated, took a breath, then said, "We are in a dangerous position." He was never one for heaping on words—even as a speaker in the Little Rock Debating Society, he rarely used all of his allotted time. "The government is splintered. We can expect nothing from it, sir. Respectfully, I think those men aren't focused on what matters. They have become distracted and are fighting personal battles while dreaming of conquests beyond their capabilities." He relaxed his shoulders and ended his statement with, "As such, they're likely to be as much help to us as are the gunmen living back in Tennessee. We must make do on our own."

Neill turned to him, and Jesse feared he might have been too candid after all, for the colonel's face was dark and grim.

"We must make do on our own," Neill slowly repeated and returned to his desk, still well-supplied with writing paper.

"After a day's rest, sir, I can be ready to ride out again as needed," Jesse assured him.

Neill shook his head and said, "No, I need you here for a while."

"Now, Jesse, go sup, find your new quarters, and get some rest. I must read these letters and collect my thoughts. Report to me here in the morning."

"Yes, sir."

Jesse started to leave, but Neill's voice came again at his back, and he turned at the door.

"You did well in San Felipe. Be attentive to what you hear among the men. I would like to know their minds, too."

Jesse took pride in the approval of his commanding officer, nodding as he said "Thank you, Colonel Neill," and left the office to find a bunk and something to eat other than flatbread and preserved venison. In the twilight, he took a walk around the interior grounds of the Alamo, refamiliarizing himself with the fort and looking for some fellowship. He found Major Jameson, and the two talked while the waning crescent moon rose, with the major speaking about his home in Kentucky and the private about moving from North Carolina to Tennessee with his father.

Among many things that same evening, Neill wrote a letter to the governor asking for a writ of election so that his men could send two delegates to the upcoming Convention. Since they were not considered residents of the town, they were denied permission by the civilian authorities in San Antonio to vote on February 1. This had naturally caused discontent. The men were soldiers enlisted to fight Santa Anna, their common enemy. For their service, and in accord with their understanding of liberty, they expected to be represented at the Convention. Neill thought that this was something that the Provisional Government would do to support them since it did not require money, more men, or good military strategy.[1]

After Jesse's return from San Felipe, William joined the United States Invincibles, a company commanded by Captain John M.

Chenoweth. It would garrison the port of Copano on the Gulf of Mexico. Chenoweth had, at least, received proper approval from the Provisional Government.[2]

On January 20, 1836, Chenoweth's company drew their horses in preparation for departure. Jesse and William stood beside each other, unsure of when they would do so again. Jesse placed his hand on his brother's shoulder and looked him in the eye.

"Be careful and take care of yourself. Chenoweth is a commendable leader. I hope to see you back in Little Rock when this is all over."

William embraced Jesse, simply stating "I will, Brother."

Jesse helped William tie his last rations to his mare before once again resting his hand on his brother's shoulder to say goodbye. William tipped his hat before joining the rest of the company. Jesse watched them ride until he could no longer make them out. He hoped this would not be the last time he laid eyes on the company.

There was little hard news but much rumor of the continued stand-off in San Felipe between the Council and Governor Smith, who were now both denying the other's right to lead. In the days after Jesse's return from San Felipe, some reinforcements and supplies did indeed trickle in. Thirty more men arrived led by Colonel James Bowie and Lieutenant James Bonham. A foraging party returned with a small herd of cattle, but, while the fresh beef was welcomed, it was not enough.

A driver who arrived with a small wagon full of corn said that Governor Smith had charged the Council with misusing $500.00—a gift given to Texas for the purpose of paying and resupplying the soldiers at the Alamo. The driver shared this news with Colonel Neill, the soldiers who helped him unload, and a group gathered around a low flame waiting for their thin, pale excuse for coffee to boil. Soon the entire garrison knew of the Council's transgression.[3]

Jesse briefly feared that this news could turn the trickle of deserters into a flood, but he realized that, since his return from San Felipe, he had felt a shift in the way the men thought. It seemed that they were no longer just a collection of individuals. They were not as disciplined as regular troops in the United States Army, but they worked together like a group of men with a common goal. They had been invigorated by the arrival of Jim Bowie, though much of the credit for their work and spirits was due to the leadership of Colonel Neill. Most of all, the men of the Alamo had a determination to see their mission through.

The arrival of Bowie's men and horses provided Neill the resources to send out scouting patrols to assess the movement of the enemy. Several thousand men of the Mexican Army were said to be gathering with the intent to attack Copano and Goliad, but a detachment of a few hundred marched north to retake Bexar.

After seven days, Neill had no response to his letter about the election of delegates to the Convention. Although a week was barely enough time to expect a reply from San Felipe, Neill wrote another letter regarding the issuance of a writ:

> *Dear Sir,*
>
> *I ask the privilege of you to send to me here at this place a Writ of Election for the Volunteer Army now under my command to authorize them to Elect two delegates to the Convention to be held in Washington. The reasons I request this is not a man here under my command will can have a voice only by and through that method they are all volunteers they are in favor of independence.*
>
> *Such men should be represented in the council of their country and that too by men chosen from among themselves. The Citizens have all declared for us and will on the 1st day of next month take the oath to support the provisional govt. You have the highest regards of the whole army and you shall be sustained for your firmness and philanthropy.*
>
> *Yours in haste.*
>
> *J.C. Neill, Lt. Col.*
>
> *Commandant of Bexar*[4]

He let his efforts be known among the men so that they knew their commander had them on his mind.

The next day, Neill invited Jesse to walk with him from the Alamo into San Antonio. In the civic square, Jesse noted that it was strangely quiet for midday.

"Families in the town are scattering," Neill told him. "John Smith has packed up his whole clan into a caravan and headed north to the colonies where it's safe." He shook his head. "Several good working men—white and Tejano—have gone to God knows where. They were working with the beeves, but there was no money to pay them, so I reckon that they have cut their losses. The volunteers have not been paid in two months. A few of them have left as well."

"I still have some money, colonel, and I could help in that way."

"Thank you, Jesse," he said putting his hand on the private's shoulder. "I may accept your offer later, but for now I need your help in a different way. We must impress on the Council how their failure to act and their follies are seen by the soldiers who are here to defend them from Santa Anna. They risk their lives out here while they fiddle back there. And we need the men to understand that I am not fiddling. I am fighting for them."

Neill outlined his plan to call a political meeting of the soldiers, like the town hall meetings they were used to back in the United States. At the meeting, he would appoint a committee to write a preamble and resolutions and set out their grievances for a vote by the assembly.

"These men must be heard. They need to air their grievances, and they need to know that their concerns have been written down and sent to the Council. I want to support Henry and Sam and let the Council know the depth of feeling here against them. The Council must come to its senses and do the right thing or else we will fail."

His commander sounded as if he were trying to convince himself that a meeting with resolutions would make a difference with the Council, when, in fact, he knew that it would not. The effect on morale, however, could be substantial.

"I want you to represent the private soldiers on that committee."

Jesse clasped his hands behind his back and walked on with Neill in silence, thinking about what this meant and the importance of the task.

"Colonel Neill, I am honored, sir, by your confidence in me. I can do this. I was there in San Felipe when the Government lost its way."

"Excellent," said Neill, slapping his hip for emphasis. "Keep your selection to yourself until I announce it, but speak with Dr. Pollard and Major Jameson. Learn all that you can to inform your conduct." That afternoon, Neill announced the meeting for January 26, so talk was everywhere—and Jesse was a good listener.

Jesse had the eerie sensation that time was of the essence. For the next two days, he worked alongside his fellow soldiers as they prepared for battle. They moved earth to dig trenches and embankments and used logs and lumber to construct cover and concealment for gun crews. They dug wells and positioned water barrels and ammunition for quick access. They inspected their magazines to be certain that their powder was dry.

He met in the late evenings with Neill to discuss what he had heard, which included complaints about not being allowed to vote in the election. "I am aware and will address the election issue in its time," Neill told him. On the immediate topic, Jesse asked, "And what if we have no answer to our resolves?" They had become comfortable enough with each other to speak with increasing candor and engagement.

Neill smiled at him wryly. "Then, we must make do," he said.

On January 26, Jesse attended the assembly, was called out by Colonel Neill to serve, and sat on the committee with six others to draft a formal condemnation of the acts of the Council and declare their support for Governor Smith and General Houston. On the committee with Jesse were Major Jameson and Dr. Pollard, as well as Bowie and Lieutenant Bonham and local leaders Captain Juan Nepomuceno Sequin and Don Gaspar Flores de Abrego.

Since the goal was to have a document for the assembly to approve, there was a rough draft already available to be discussed in committee and presented for a vote before the men got restless and drifted away. Nevertheless, they edited the work, agreeing to use direct, unequivocal language and to open with a description of events as they saw and understood them. Jesse's perspective from the events in San Felipe was alluded to in the first line.

> *Whereas we have been informed from an undoubted messenger, that the executive council and its president, a subordinate and auxiliary department of the government, have usurped the right of impeaching the governor, whom if we would imitate the wise institutions of the land of Washington, can only be impeached by a body set forth in the Constitution...*

They went on to detail the malfeasances of the Council, though there was some disagreement on whether to include a complaint about the $500.00 that had failed to come their way. Bonham argued that to mention money made them seem insincere about their democratic convictions. Others insisted that it be put on record lest the whole crooked business be swept away after the Convention, their service not only unpaid but forgotten. Accordingly, in the fourth resolution regarding the money, they emphasized their dedication and their sincere belief in the cause behind the army they volunteered for, firmly distinguishing themselves from mercenaries or filibusters.

> *Resolved 4th: That the conduct of the president and members of the executive council in relation to the five hundred dollar loan, for the liquidation of the claims of the soldiers in Bexar, is the highest degree criminal and unjust; Yet under the moment however illiberal and ungrateful, we cannot be driven from the post of honor—and the sacred cause of Freedom.*

The finished document consisted of a preamble and seven resolutions, a modest statement in comparison to some, but Jesse was pleased with how it came together and the impression he felt it gave. The assembly agreed by voice vote.[5]

"These Resolves set out our grievances and have been approved by you men so that the General Councilors in San Felipe must read your words!" Neill thundered at the close of the meeting.

Supported by three "huzzahs" from the men, Colonel Neill folded the document along with a note from himself affirming that it had been voted on and approved in assembly as the resolutions of the army at Bexar.

He sent an express with the original to the Council with copies for the editors of the *Brazoria Gazette*, the *Nacogdoches Telegraph*, and the *San Felipe Telegraph*.

The next day, Jesse was summoned to Neill's office.

"Damn them for failing us. This would've cost them nothing but a sheet of paper," Neill growled with some heat, after noting that he still had no word from San Felipe about an election writ. "Jesse, I've decided that we will have an election and send two delegates to the Convention. We will vote regardless of what I may later hear from the Provisional Government. I will force the Convention itself to seat our men or turn them away and close the door on them."

Jesse felt a rush of respect for his commander, as he had hoped that this would be Neill's direction after the events of the past few days.

"Jesse, I want to nominate you for election as one of two delegates."

This announcement came as a shock, and Jesse asked why Neill had picked him over one of the officers.

Neill explained to Jesse why he was a natural choice for a delegate. He had the proper skills and experience for this task, and he had no skills or experience in military matters.

"I'm certain that you are a fine marksman, Jesse, but you're more useful to us at the Convention than on the walls. You did well in San Felipe with Henry and the Council. You did well on the Resolves Committee working with Bowie and Bonham. And I know that you believe in our cause and want to win independence as we all do here."

Jesse could scarcely believe in his prospects of being among the men who would declare the independence of a new nation, wrested separate and free from an authoritarian ruler worse than George III. His grandfather had supported the American Revolution, but did not attain so high a place as Jesse now had in his grasp.

Of course, he realized, he must first win the election—and the

Convention must vote for independence—but, somehow, he felt confident of both events.

Determined not to disappoint Neill, who, nineteen years his senior, had honored him with his trust, Jesse thanked his commanding officer and pledged that he would not let his fellow soldiers down.

9

THE ALAMO DELEGATE

In the absence of a writ of election from the Provisional Government, Lieutenant Colonel Neill announced that he and other officers of the garrison would sign a petition directed to the Convention for two delegates from the Alamo to be seated. He would hold an election on the date selected by the Consultation for authorized elections, February 1, and he would nominate Jesse B. Badgett and Dr. Samuel Augustus Maverick as candidates.

The men respected Neill and took his intended nominations under thoughtful consideration. Jesse was never much for politicking, but he made an extra effort to listen to the soldiers. Volunteers from the Siege and capture of San Antonio complained about not getting paid as promised. Many of them groused about the lack of proper food and equipment, blaming their plight on Grant, Johnson, and the Council. They all supported Governor Smith, the matters advanced in the Resolves, and independence for Texas.

Dr. Pollard argued that a newly-independent Texas should forbid slavery. While there were some who seemed moved by his words, as Jesse predicted, the abolitionist was very much in the minority. A few men engaged him with philosophical questions like those he had argued in the debating society, ranging from freedom of religion to whether there should be debtors' prisons.

While the work went ahead on the fortifications, the election gave the men a common focus that proved to be an antidote to fear, hunger, privation, illness, and injury. All of them were animated by the thought of winning a war for independence from the dictator, Santa Anna, and looked forward to living on their bounty land in Texas after the war.

On the date appointed, the soldiers gathered in the courtyard of the Alamo. Each soldier could vote for two different men. The votes were not cast in secret but were counted by election judges who recorded the name of each voter and the names of the men for whom he voted. Jesse and Maverick were nominated by Lieutenant Colonel Neill. John H. Hayes and Lieutenant Bonham were nominated by JH Nash.

Despite their situation, the men were buoyant as they gathered to vote. Food had been growing scarcer and rations smaller. Most of the men were clad in what they could make do with threadbare linen shirts and pants stiff from many days of hard work without laundry. Tension had made some men short-tempered and brusque; nevertheless, the dignity granted by suffrage had given them a sense of voice and control in their destinies, and they were eager for the proceedings.

Jesse had smoothed back his dark hair and unkempt beard in an attempt to appear more presentable for the formal proceedings of an election. As he looked around, he found that nearly every man returned his look directly into his eyes. Some men regarded him openly with a small, serious smile. He took this to mean that Neill's assessment of how the election would go was correct. Jesse cast a single vote for Dr. Maverick, who, in turn, voted only for Jesse. From a total of 104 voters, Maverick garnered 103 votes with Jesse only three behind him at 100. The other two candidates, Hayes and Bonham, received one vote each from JH Nash. Three soldiers voted only for Maverick.[1]

The tension at the fort grew more each day. The men worked long days to improve the fortifications and gun emplacements, but they were still uncertain whether they would be joined by reinforcements, be ordered to abandon the Alamo to combine with some larger force, or be left to face an overwhelming enemy on their own.

On the morning of February 3, Lieutenant Colonel William Barrett Travis arrived with 23 soldiers of the regular Army of Texas. As regulars, they carried themselves in a more disciplined manner. Their arrival was a welcomed boost to the garrison in both number and morale.

The next day, Neill noted that he had still received no money from the Provisional Government and asked Jesse for a loan of $50.00 to pay some of the old volunteers from the Siege. Jesse enthusiastically advanced the cash. He felt engaged in the revolution that was unfolding around him and was grateful to play a larger role. He almost felt as if he were living a dream.[2]

More good news arrived on February 8 when former Tennessee Congressman David Crockett arrived at the post with a few men from Tennessee. Crockett was a well-known name along the frontier, and the soldiers were eager to have him among them. Instantly seeing the advantages to morale, Neill invited him to speak to the men, and Crockett stood on top of a box to do so. His arrival and service as a private soldier made some of the men feel invincible, since surely a man of his stature would not throw in his lot with theirs unless he was certain that they were doing the right thing. Later, Jesse spoke amiably with Crockett about Tennessee and introduced himself as the nephew of two of Crockett's many friends and political supporters back in Tennessee. Two days after Crockett's arrival, Neill hosted a fandango in his honor. Crockett played his fiddle to the delight of all.

The days continued to rush forward. One afternoon, Jesse returned to Neill's headquarters after a meager midday meal of tamales and beans to find his commander pale and in the grip of strong emotions. Jesse asked what news had affected him so much. He held his breath waiting for a response, expecting from Neill's demeanor to hear that the Mexican Army would be arriving in the next hour or the next day. "Express news from home," Neill slowly answered, "There is sickness in my house and my family calls me to return immediately."

Worried and thinking that he had the time to make the round-trip journey before Santa Anna could threaten the Alamo, Neill decided to take a leave of absence. After a night's hectic preparation, he rode out of the fort on February 11.

Among his last acts as he left the Alamo, Neill endorsed Jesse's expenses to be paid at the Convention. These expenses included the eleven-day express ride to San Felipe and back, the use of his own horse, the purchase of supplies for the hospital, the purchase of paper for headquarters, and the $50.00 loan for the pay of the soldiers. Neill also signed off on the petition asking the Convention to seat both Jesse and Maverick as delegates.

"Jesse, before I leave, I will discharge you from your obligation to the army."

"Colonel, I need three more days to get the bounty land. Could I stay here until the fourteenth and get the 90 days of service?" Neill reluctantly agreed to Jesse's request, but admonished him not to tarry since he did not want to risk depriving the garrison of his voice at the Convention if he met unexpected delays on the trail.

Jesse fervently promised to get to the convention on time, assuring him that he and Athena could easily make such a ride. Neill signed the papers dated to become effective on February 14.[3]

In the Colonel's absence, other matters delayed Jesse's departure even further. Although Neill had left Travis in command of the regulars and the enlisted volunteers, two companies of old volunteers from the Siege who were used to electing their own commanders refused to serve under Travis. Instead, after some agitation by Bowie, they elected him as their leader. Jesse saw the dispute as a threat to the work that Neill had done to unite the men. As an enlisted volunteer, he was obligated to serve under Travis' command and did not consider following Bowie any more than he had considered following Grant instead of Neill.

After his election as commander of two volunteer companies, Bowie got drunk, stayed drunk, tried to assume command of the entire garrison, and interfered with the administration of civil law in San Antonio. Jesse was not impressed.

"That man Bowie acts little better than Grant and those men on the Council. They are all smart and have some skills, but they think too much of themselves," Jesse said, discussing the matter with Dr. Pollard and Major Jameson. They agreed that Jesse should stay to support Travis until the situation had settled down, a decision that Lieutenant Colonel Travis approved. Then, almost as quickly as it had started, the matter settled with an agreement between Travis and Bowie to share command.

As he prepared to leave, Jesse was visited by Captain Samuel Blair. A regular Texas Army officer from Tennessee, Blair was the same age as Jesse. Indeed, they had met when Blair lived in Conway County, Arkansas. He came to Texas in 1834 as a settler first in Power and Hewetson's Colony and then in McGloin's Colony. On February 1, he had been an election judge and signed Jesse's certificate of election as a delegate. He was a veteran of the Siege of Bexar and the fort's Assistant Ordnance Chief.

He ostensibly found Jesse to wish him safe travels to the Convention, but Jesse sensed that there was some reason more pressing for the captain's visit. Working up to the question, Blair asked if Jesse would consider buying an assignment of his military pay.

"I can spend the money here and now to buy food for the men and to get our laundry done," said Blair. "You can get reimbursed at the Convention, but I don't think that a paymaster will be coming here to pay me. Anyway, these men are like family now."[4]

When Jesse finally departed on February 17, he left behind two bottles of wine and three pounds of gunpowder, for which he got a receipt signed by Travis, who also gave him dispatches and letters to deliver. He also carried Travis's red Morocco-bound expense account book requesting reimbursement for Travis of $143.00 from the government. Travis also approved an assignment by Captain Blair of his military pay to Jesse.[5]

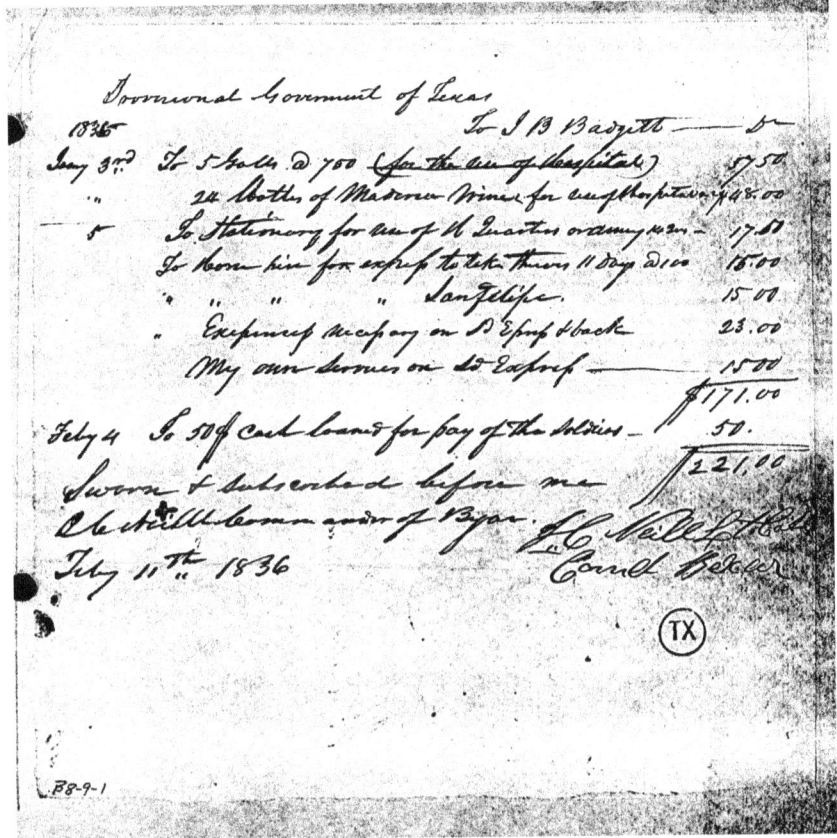

Jesse's expense report

Though he felt a pang of guilt, it was an undeniable relief to be away from the conditions of the fort and to be on his own again, even in the frigid nights of mid-winter. It was a new moon, so there would be no moonlit nocturnal travel. He would have to camp each day before sundown, but he had plenty of time.

The landscape and sky of Texas—God's magnificent creation— offered Jesse a warm and comforting embrace in which he found a peaceful beauty after the tension and activity of confined, man-made spaces. Nevertheless, he knew that this time alone was only a brief respite before he arrived at the Convention, which would have a potent energy of its own. He had observed and discussed the proceedings of the Territorial Legislature in Little Rock, so he had an idea about what was to come.

Accordingly, Jesse made the most of this interlude to reflect upon what he had learned and what he had to do, but these thoughts were constantly interrupted by concern for his brother William. Where was he now? Did he make it to Copano? The brothers had grown so close since leaving Tennessee that he acutely felt William's absence.

Jesse allowed himself to be selective in his campsites, sheltering against natural bluffs to block the wind when he could. He passed up the shelter of scattered dogtrot cabins along the way, preferring to be in the open air with Athena, his thoughts, and a good fire. The weather was mild during the day, and, even in the darkest part of night, it was not as cold as it had been back in that horrible January of 1832. Lying on his back at night, he got lost in the heavens.

Sitting in his saddle by day, he faced an unblemished vista. The roads that men built here simply could not impose their order on this land as they did back in Maury County, Tennessee. He stopped in one empty stretch to hunt for jackrabbit, then let Athena take up the road at a comfortable pace. By evening, he moved forward more rapidly, anxious to find his next campsite and build a cooking fire before sundown.

He passed quickly through San Felipe and rode north along the Brazos River to Washington, where he arrived with plenty of time to establish himself. He found the town to be a loose collection of homes, stores, and warehouses upon a bluff. It sat a short distance down a road leading away from the Robinson and Hall ferry crossing of the Brazos River. As Jesse approached, he saw that horses were set to graze on a nearby prairie and set Athena to join the other steeds. He felt comfortable here in a familiar, wooden world instead of the stone and adobe of the Spanish settlements.

Having taken care of Athena, Jesse looked for food and lodging. Everything in the small town was expensive and crowded, but he found a room to share and some North American cooking to eat. He liked most Mexican food well enough but missed the more familiar taste of fried chicken and biscuits. He took a bath, had his laundry done, and bought a simple new shirt but could find no trousers for sale. He rested before exploring further.

The town was crowded with men from the United States, several of whom he had already met in Texas. Elected Convention delegates and men from the Provisional Government were all to chart the future course of Texas. There were also men who were attracted to centers of power in hope of appointed office, government contracts, or land.

There was a great deal of talk, and much of the news was grim. Jesse had received no word from his brother since he had departed with the Invincibles. He asked two men from Copano for news of William and learned that he had left that place with a detachment for Refugio. He later smiled to learn from another delegate that, while Jesse was being elected at the Alamo, his brother was presiding as an election judge in Refugio. Another delegate reported that William had left Refugio with Colonel James Walker Fannin's mounted relief force, which was now at Goliad, and headed down the Gonzales Road to reinforce the Alamo.[6]

Jesse briefly wished he had delayed his departure to see his brother again before the war escalated further. He took comfort in knowing William would surely hear news of him when he arrived at the Alamo. While William fought the despot, Jesse would work with free men to build a functional, democratic government.

The building that would house the Convention was unfinished, with no doors or windows against the cold, early-morning air. In lieu of glass, sheets of cotton were stretched over the windows. It was a long wooden structure with four small rooms and a large central chamber. Long tables and benches stretched from end to end, and chairs with lap desks sat loosely grouped in corners.

Entering this building for the first time the day before their proceedings, Jesse found a group of delegates gathered behind an aristocratic, Mexican man. He was seated at a table with a large and intricate map laid out in front of him, the corners held in place by books. Another stack of books sat in the chair next to him. The man spoke with an articulate voice as he described the likely movements of Santa Anna's troops, certainly based on his knowledge of the Mexican forces and terrain they must cross. Jesse joined the others and listened intently to the man's analysis, impressed with how much clarity he gave to what had been a confused muddle of differing reports. After the gentleman was done, and the group dispersed, Jesse introduced himself and found the man was Lorenzo de Zavala, a politician from the Yucatan of national and international experience.[7]

On February 29, Jesse met with the disbursement officer to receive his military pay, reimbursement for his expenses, and for the assignment of Captain Blair's pay. While there was no money at the Alamo, there seemed to be enough in Washington.[8]

That night, the weather changed abruptly when a blue norther swept in with freezing temperatures. Jesse reflected on whether this was an omen.

The next day, March 1, the Convention commenced, beginning with the examination of the delegates' election credentials. He was ready to defend the right of his constituents to elect delegates, but the petition and certification signed by the officers were not challenged. It helped that other soldiers in the field had sent delegates as well.

Jesse took a seat next to two delegates elected by the civilians of Bexar—Jose Francisco Ruiz and his nephew, Jose Antonio Navarro. These two men were the only native-born Tejanos among the delegates at the Convention. Ruiz was a politician and a soldier who had been active in the Mexican War of Independence against the autocratic and incompetent King Ferdinand VII, and he likewise opposed Santa Anna. Navarro was a politician and a merchant who had joined the Texas Revolution with his uncle. Jesse's fellow delegate from the Alamo had not yet arrived.[9]

After all delegates had taken their seats, an attorney from Nashville, Tennessee, George Campbell Childress, called the meeting to order and moved the election of a Convention president. Richard Ellis was unanimously elected and spoke to them of the importance of their duties and how they were following the great example of the American colonies a hundred years prior. Other key positions in the

Convention were filled, including the appointment of five men to a committee for drafting a declaration of independence for their consideration and signatures. Well begun, the Convention adjourned for the following day.[10]

On March 2, the delegates reconvened and established rules for order, debate, and procedure. Then the committee for drafting a declaration gave their report. The speed with which they had worked led Jesse to think that a draft declaration had been brought to the Convention, but no objection was raised, and no man murmured or allowed his chair legs to scrape the rough wooden floor as the report was read. It began:

> When a government has ceased to protect the lives, liberty and property of the people, from whom its legitimate powers are derived, and for the advancement of whose happiness it was institute—

The Declaration went on to tell the colonists' story of Texas: how settlers had come, feeling secure under the protection of the Mexican Constitution of 1824 that was so similar to that of their neighboring homeland, and how that constitution was disregarded under the tyrant Santa Anna. It told of their impossible choice—to abandon the homes they had built through labor and sacrifice or to submit to "the most intolerable of all tyranny, the combined despotism of the sword and the priesthood." It listed the ways in which Santa Anna had abused the powers of the military. It contended that the right to abolish a failed government and to establish another was invariably connected to the first law of nature—self-preservation.

The report concluded:

> We, therefore, the delegates, with plenary powers, of the people of Texas, in solemn convention assembled, appealing to a candid world for the necessities of our condition, do hereby resolve and declare that our political connexion with the Mexican nation has forever ended; and that the people of Texas do now constitute a free, sovereign and independent Republic, and are fully invested with all the rights and attributes which properly belong

to independent nations; and conscious of the rectitude of our intentions, we fearlessly and confidently commit the issue to the supreme arbiter of the destinies of nations.

The reader of the report lowered the pages, and the room shook with applause and shouts of affirmation from the forty-four gathered men. When the clamor finally subsided, the men were called back to order, and, upon motion, the report was unanimously received and adopted. The delegates added a caption: "The unanimous Declaration of Independence made by the Delegates of the People of Texas, in General-Convention at the town of Washington, on the 2nd day of March, 1836." The working copy required more work before an official copy would be ready to sign, and a small ceremony was slated for the following day. Questions of printing and distribution were also settled before the convention adjourned for a midday recess.

During this break, Jesse found a quiet moment in which to write to his brother, Noah, back in Little Rock. He could scarcely believe that it had been only a few months since he had left Little Rock, for more seemed to have happened in these mere dozen weeks than in the years of his life before. As he wrote to Noah of his role in the Convention and the events at the Alamo that led him there, it occurred to him that he would forever consider his life as divided on these days.

That evening, an express courier arrived from Travis, and the dispatch was relayed to the Convention. A force of three hundred Mexican soldiers had attacked the Alamo, using the nearby abandoned houses for cover. After a cannonade, the defenders held the attacking force at bay.

Jesse could picture the skirmish clearly, having made a tour of the mounted cannon positions with Neill and Jameson. Only three Texians were wounded; none were killed. A sighing sound could be heard in the room at this news. What the men from Refugio had told him earlier that day was confirmed: Colonel Fannin was on the march from Goliad with three hundred and fifty men. The consensus among the delegates was that Fannin would have likely reached the

Alamo by now, and, with other forces on the way, soon the fort would be protected by six or seven hundred soldiers, his brother William among them. It was believed that the Alamo would be safe for now.[11]

I Saml C Blair do Solemny Swore that the dis
Charge that I have this day Transferd to Jesse
C Badgett Signed by P H Blair and Counter
Signed by Edward Burleson Commander
in Chief and boring date as per discharge
Heror by Transferd and that this is the only
Discharge that I have Received from any officer
or officers of the Feddural Volluntere army
of Texas and that I have never Transferd
Said Claim to any Persons or Persons Except
Said Badgett is the auley Person authorised
to draw Said money for me and in My
name and in the name of my hiers and
assigns from the Proper orthorities of the
State and Reupt to the Provitional
Goverment prior any other that may hear
after be Established for the Same and
further that Said Government or armey has
No Claim or debt against me what Ever
for a valuable Consideration which is
Endorsed on Said descharge Born Feby 17
1836 Swore to and Subscribed before me

(TX)

M P Travis
Lt Cool cavalry

Blair's charge to Jesse

PART III

10

THE CALL AND THE FALL

The delegates could see their breath as they reconvened in the hall at nine the next morning, Thursday, March 3. As the sun began to shine in earnest and the air grew warmer, the men began to discard their coats. The first item of business was to sign the engrossed Declaration. They were called to sign the document alphabetically by the name of the place that had elected them. Ruiz, Navarro, and Jesse signed together for "Bexar." After he signed, he looked around the room and then back down at his signature on the document, feeling the weight of their decision and wanting to implant the moment solidly in his memory.

That afternoon, Jesse was appointed to a committee of twenty-two delegates to organize the physical force of the new country's defenses. Zavala was also on this committee, and Jesse continued to be impressed by his sharp mind and commanding presence. For the rest of that first week, questions of some elections were resolved, a regiment of rangers was formed, and Sam Houston was appointed commander in chief of the armies of Texas. Motions were made, and most passed without question or reserve; what debate there was had been civil and resolved in a matter of course. The only time raised voices threatened to become heated was regarding the split and rancor between the General Council and the former governor of the Provisional Government. Even this fury was set aside in favor of pushing forward towards resolution.

The Convention adjourned Friday evening with the intent to reconvene and begin drafting a constitution that Monday.

Jesse grew to know the two native-born Tejanos from Bexar, Navarro and Ruiz, though their acquaintanceship felt acutely the barrier between their different native tongues. The smattering of Spanish words Jesse had acquired those past few months were inadequate for more than the simplest communication, and they each spoke a broken English that was only marginally better than Jesse's Spanish. They relied heavily on a couple men acting as translators including Zavala, who was fluent and eloquent in both languages and could easily switch between the two in conversation.[1]

The additional temporary population strained the small town's resources, crowding into only one small boarding house run by Marshall and Pamelia Mann and a tavern operated by Mr. Roberts. How to comfortably house the members of the Convention for the duration of their work became a hot topic, with some sleeping in the convention hall, wrapped tightly against the bitter cold that came in through the cotton window coverings.[2]

That Sunday morning, March 6, the delegates were called to gather for an emergency session. As Jesse entered the main hall, he spotted Dr. Maverick. "At last, he is here," thought Jesse, and he moved toward him to hear news of the fort and to discover what had kept him, but before Jesse had a chance to speak, President Ellis called for order. Ellis explained that he convened the session to hear some urgent news that required action by the Convention.

A letter and messenger had arrived from Travis. The letter was dated for February 24 and painted a drastically darker picture than what they had heard earlier that week. Though the weather had been warming each day, a chill settled over Jesse as he listened to the letter read out:

To the People of Texas & All Americans in the World-

Fellow Citizens & compatriots-

I am besieged, by a thousand or more of the Mexicans under Santa Anna - I have sustained a continual Bombardment & cannonade for 24 hours & have not lost a man - The enemy has demanded a surrender at discretion, otherwise, the garrison are to be put to the sword, if the fort is taken - I have answered the demand with a cannon shot, & our flag still waves proudly from the walls - I shall never surrender or retreat. Then, I call on you in the name of Liberty, of patriotism & everything dear to the American character, to come to our aid, with all dispatch - The enemy is receiving reinforcements daily & will no doubt increase to three or four thousand in four or five days. If this call is neglected, I am determined to sustain myself as long as possible & die like a soldier who never forgets what is due to his own honor & that of his country - **Victory or Death.**

William Barret Travis

Lt. Col. Comdt

This call to arms was brought by a messenger who had escaped the Siege and added his own observations to the report, describing a small band of reinforcements, but nothing like the three-hundred and fifty that had been expected from Fannin. He gave an account of the remaining supplies—much depleted since Jesse had left the fort and only suitable for a matter of days. It was also suspected that Santa Anna himself had arrived with the company that held siege to the fort.

There was a great deal of commotion as this news was relayed to the Convention, leading one delegate to shout, "Where are our rifles?" Many seemed ready to abandon their seats and ride to the Alamo.

At this critical moment, Houston stood up and spoke calmly and deliberately at length about how their small number could not affect the military outcome even if they arrived in time, thus settling the delegates and re-focusing them on their indispensable political work. Impressed by his command of the men, Jesse thought, "So this is why men follow Houston." General Houston then left to lead the army.

For the delegates, there was nothing to be done but see to it that the purpose of the Convention be completed.

Jesse asked the messenger about his brother and other men he knew at the Alamo. When he asked about how the shared command was working, he learned that Bowie had taken ill and conceded all command authority to Travis. While he regretted Bowie's illness, a unified command was a positive development. He was disturbed to learn that there had been no money, horses, or supplies sent to the fort, nor had an adequate number of fighting men arrived.[3]

The next morning, March 7, the Convention began in earnest to draft a constitution. They met continuously in committee and settled matters such as opening diplomatic relations with the United States, the Cherokee, and the Comanche, establishing land titles and commissioners, and reporting the actions of the Provisional Government. They also discussed how to resolve continued disputes and the establishment of militia forces. It was the most tedious work that Jesse had ever experienced, and the urgency of their task was at odds with the need to compromise among disparate interests, delicacy, and precision in their language.[4]

On March 8, Jesse served on a committee to ask the Provisional Government officials for information about officers in the Regular Army. On another committee, he asked the same men to turn over the government's archives to the Convention, and, on his motion, a report was received. He felt grateful to have made actionable headway on the Convention's resolutions.[5]

By Wednesday, it came as a great relief that Jesse had secured more agreeable lodging. Mr. William Fairfax Gray had successfully concluded negotiations with Samuel Heath to convert his carpentry shop into lodgings. An attorney from Virginia representing real estate investors, Gray was not a delegate but simply an interested observer of the Convention. The shop stood on the main road between the warehouses and in convenient proximity to Mr. Robert's tavern. Heath put down a new floor in the building to make it suitable for sleeping mats, and there were tables at which to write and work. Gray had arranged to rent the building for $25, and he split the cost and shared the accommodation with Jesse, Navarro, Ruiz, and Zavala.[6]

Gray was an amusing man, and a bit odd in manner. He held a pleasant disposition towards his lodging mates, particularly Zavala with whom he worked to learn what he could of Spanish, seeking out lessons in the odd times they were away from the bustle of the hall. Navarro and Ruiz seemed amused by Gray's earnest efforts, and, though they tried to correct his pronunciation as kindly as they could, they quickly gave up the effort and left it to Zavala, whose command of English allowed him to have a great deal more patience with Gray's efforts.

At all times Gray kept a journal which he updated with diligent and continuous notes of his observations, lists of Spanish words he had learned in his lessons, and any and all possible opportunities for purchases of land from the delegates and others about the area.

The relative privacy and quiet of the carpentry shop was in contrast to the low buzz of the men working by candlelight into the night on committees at the hall, murmurs and pen scratching echoing throughout. The silence was, in part, a relief, but it also allowed Jesse's thoughts to wander into unwanted speculation and fear.

There had been no further word from the Alamo, and questions about its fate hung over the convention like a brooding omnipresence. Was it assumed that they were cut off completely by siege if they had not been overrun? There was no word from General Houston, either, who was thought to be back with the army. Jesse did not know if his brother, who had been among those headed to the Alamo as relief, was fighting from inside the besieged fort or somewhere else in the open. Lying on his sleeping mat, it was too easy to wonder if their food had run out or their munitions depleted, or if a wall had been breached allowing the Mexican Army to pour in and slaughter the garrison. Already, some delegates among themselves speculated the Alamo had long since fallen and the enemy would already be marching in their direction. Zavala had been quiet on the subject during the past two days, and Jesse wondered if he was keeping his predictions to himself out of strategic tact, avoiding another call to arms before their task was properly done.

It was not until March 15 that the delegates learned the unthinkable truth of the Alamo, but, even then, Jesse had no real answers. Rumors of hope had come that morning, but so circuitously that few gave them much credit. Finally, news came from General Houston that the Alamo had fallen on the morning of March 6. Ruiz and Navarro received a separate missive in their own language that gave a corresponding report. The word was that all defenders were dead.

The news cast a deep shadow over the delegates. Voices that had been rising in pitch over the questions of land grants and government loans calmed and lowered. There was a great sense of loss, and not just from those who had family that might now lie dead. Jesse was thunderstruck. The presumed dead not only consisted perhaps of his brother William but all his new comrades and the men he represented at the Convention. Their names and faces flashed through his head one after another. Shock and denial were quickly followed by anger, and grief began to weigh heavily upon him.

The convention officially adjourned until the morning of the sixteenth, but, after a simple supper of roast pork and potatoes, the delegates seemed reluctant to depart the hall. The Alamo had fallen nine days ago, which meant that the Mexican Army was surely advancing to the northeast. A shared sense of loss and immediate danger prompted a resolve to complete their work. The Convention was hardly well-protected. Already, there were urgent whispers about crossing the Brazos to put more distance and a natural barrier between themselves and Santa Anna's forces.

The delegates unanimously agreed to reconvene and work into the night with the understanding that they could not abandon the place without setting up an interim government and finishing its constitution. They returned to the question that was left undecided before dinner regarding how new counties would be established in the independent Republic of Texas. It was clear that they were quickly growing impatient with questions of such bureaucracy, but it was the very work that needed to be done. Texas had already learned hard lessons about how split and ill-structured governments could lead to inaction in their most crucial moments. They were determined not to allow such discord to happen again, for if it did, Texas would surely fall before it really stood.[7]

Wednesday the sixteenth was a chaotic day in the convention hall, as the central disputes that had been quietly brewing over the two weeks came to a head. Urgent military decisions collided with policies that would set the law of the land. The discussions were further complicated by delegates who wanted to find their families and flee the advancing Mexican Army.

Mr. Gray observed these proceedings with increasing sourness, though his primary concern centered on the matter of land, policy, and large loans and their use. At first, Jesse was irritated by his lodging companion's reaction to the proceedings. But as he grew to understand the man, he could see that Gray championed sensibility over matters of ego. Though he had no vote in the Convention, he did not take the chance in these final days to flee along with the others.

That evening the men gathered again after they adjourned to hear news that came late. Additional candles and lanterns were brought in, and they set back to their work. As midnight came and went, there was a final reading of the draft constitution, and it was, at long last, adopted to stand as the fundamental principles and established framework of the Texas government. Then, Jesse voted for the "Bounty Resolution" to pay each new army volunteer with Texas land.

In the early hours of the morning, the Convention unanimously elected David G. Burnett as President of the Republic of Texas and Zavala as Vice President. They elected the four essential cabinet secretaries and an attorney general. The new government officers were sworn in at four o'clock Thursday morning.

As Jesse and his lodging companions walked slowly back down the road to the carpentry shop, Gray clasped the right hand of Zavala and gave him a few sincere-sounding words in Spanish, undoubtedly congratulating him on his post. Zavala thanked him—a word even

Jesse knew. An amused exchange of looks between Ruiz and Navarro suggested Gray's attempted Spanish was not quite correct.[8]

The delegates reconvened mid-morning and were working towards settling some of the final questions when the rapid pounding of hooves could be heard on the road—a single rider passing through town at a disrespectful speed. The delegates fell quiet and turned to the noise. Soon there was shouting as well. Jesse and a dozen others left the hall to find the source of the commotion and saw a rider barreling up the road toward the ferry crossing. The man's shouts clarified into words as he passed the hall. "Mexican Army is moving east! Enemy cavalry crossing at Bastrop!" Several men approached the road's edge and waived their arms at the man to interrogate him for more thorough news, but the rider would not be delayed, his eyes intent on the river crossing ahead. He merely repeated his message: "Mexican Army is moving east! Enemy cavalry crossing at Bastrop!"

Mr. Blair, a man of the town, had come to the road to hear the rider as well, and he went pale as the man's words hit him. He turned from the road at a run and started hollering the names of his wife and two children. Another delegate that was new to Texas turned to Jesse and asked him "How far is Bastrop from here?"

"Sixty-five, maybe seventy-five miles," Jesse answered him grimly.

The delegates returned to the hall with renewed urgency. Disputes began to resolve more quickly, and they settled what matters they could and assigned responsibility for remaining issues to the newly elected leaders.

The convention then adjourned, but Jesse still had work to do for Texas. He had volunteered to take copies of the Declaration and The Bounty Resolution back to Little Rock and drum up support for the revolution.

The lodgers in Heath's carpentry shop hurried to pack up their gear and join the crowds waiting their turn at the only ferry available to cross the river, though fetching their horses and finishing business with the departing delegates put them at the landing at different hours. Jesse had to wait for copies of the Bounty Resolution to be prepared for him, but he already had a copy of the Declaration that he had signed. Meanwhile, the ferry made continuous trips from afternoon into evening with more going east along the road all the time.

Jesse and Athena shared the ferry late that evening with a few families and Mrs. Robinson, who complained to all in earshot that her horse had been commandeered by a colonel, and that she intended to take the first unattended mare she could find. When they landed, it was drizzling, and, loathe to risk setting her free to graze, Jesse took Athena into a nearby wood to bivouac for the night.[9]

Jesse caught up with Vice President Zavala, the cabinet, Ruiz, Navarro, and Mr. Gray the following day. They encountered many people along the road, some desperate souls on foot and others in hastily-assembled wagon trains. One family was packing up a small wagon behind a lonely house. Zavala rode a stout little mule in the front of their party. He spoke to Ruiz and Navarro in his rapid, easy Spanish. Hearing their approach and the Spanish talk, a young woman turned and shrieked for her father who stumbled out of their small house, arms encumbered with pots and a kettle. Ruiz and Navarro ignored the outburst and Zavala gave the frightened family a small nod, but the party did not slow their pace. That night, Jesse shared a room once more with Zavala and company at Groce's Retreat.[10]

The next day, Jesse continued alone to meet Houston's army at Beeson's Crossing, hoping to find his brother. The sight there was astounding. Hundreds of men were at work fortifying the encampment. As he approached, the first soldiers he met took him as one of the volunteers that had been arriving in droves by the hour. Jesse acquitted them of the notion and explained that he came from the Convention with news for General Houston, and he sought news about his brother, William Badgett, for whose status he feared. The soldier did not know of William, but directed him to where he could find General Houston.

Jesse had to wait some time before meeting with Houston, who could only grant him moments between preparations for the war. He gratefully accepted the copy of the Bounty Resolution and asked a few questions about the final days and conclusion of the Convention. Jesse asked Houston if he had any news of those who rode with Fannin, but Houston had pressing business and directed him to an area of the camp where he could learn more about the events in Bexar.

Jesse followed the general's instructions. The camp was full of volunteers, and the mood of the encampment seemed to Jesse to be at stark odds with all those he had seen fleeing from Santa Anna. People like the Blair family from Washington were abandoning their hard-built homes with whatever they could carry in order to save their necks. All he had sensed from their faces gathering at the ferry crossing or along the road was panic and desperation. They had wanted nothing but to be free to carry on in their lives but had been forced to flee with no idea of when they could ever return or where they would be able to settle.

The volunteers here, preparing themselves for battle, had a different disposition altogether. The men shouted to each other, and everywhere was vigorous talk of seeking vengeance and victory. It was something like the fierce and resolved fortitude of the men at the Alamo. Jesse walked among the rows of tents, scanning faces for anyone familiar.

"Brother! Jesse! Jesse Badgett!"

The voice had come from behind him, and he turned to find a grinning William running to catch up to him. The brothers embraced. It had been a mere two months since they had last spoken, but it felt to Jesse like a lifetime had passed. They found a place to sit where they could hear each other, and Jesse listened intently as William recounted what had happened since they had last met.

William told how Houston was able to convince most of the men on the Matamoros Expedition to abandon that cause in favor of building a defense. Colonel Fannin led them to Goliad.

"Nathaniel? Charles?" Jesse asked.

William gravely shook his head. "They stayed with Grant and went on towards Matamoros. Charles died crossing a river before they got there and Nathaniel died in San Patricio. Johnson did not post sentries and, in the middle of the night, the Mexican Army took them. They were overpowered completely and surrendered for their lives. But you should know by now that the Mexican commanders have strict orders from Santa Anna to execute prisoners. Only a few—Johnson and a couple others—were able to get back to us. Grant was killed after being caught out in the open gathering horses."[11]

Jesse closed his eyes and lowered his head. He whispered a few words of prayer for them, words that he seemed to repeat too often as of late.

"You were right, of course, Jesse. About Matamoras," William said tersely.

Jesse shrugged and said nothing. Had his speech convinced their friends to stay at the Alamo, they still would have lost their lives.

William, seeing Jesse's downcast eyes, added, "You convinced me, Jesse. You did all you could for them."

"Did you get back to the Alamo?"

"We tried to reach it but were rebuffed at the Cibolo River. The Mexican Army had us blocked, but a group from the Alamo got out and made it to the crossing. And that is when I met David Crockett! He was their captain! Three of them rode out of the fort to the Cibolo River crossing and gathered some men and went back in through Mexican lines. It was quite something to see, Jesse. Crockett riding out of the darkness and then riding back out into the night."[12]

"Tell me, is it true? Are they all dead?"

"Yes, Jesse. All of them except a woman and her child and Travis's slave Joe. Santa Anna spared only those three."

"Did no one else escape? Was no one else spared?"

"No one. They are all gone."

Jesse said nothing, and, for a while, they hunkered together in silence.

Jesse exhaled slowly through his nose and could not think of what to say. "So," he started finally. "I shared the floor of a carpentry shop with the new Vice President of a free Texas," he said with a wry smile. He updated William on the happenings of the Convention. As he spoke, it was clear William was not as keen on the details of the proceedings as Jesse had been to hear William's news.

When he came to the end of his account, William asked if Jesse had been posted to a new unit.

Jesse shook his head.

"Well, I'm sure we can arrange for you to fight—"

Jesse shook his head again. "No, I am not staying. I was discharged from the army to attend the Convention."

William's eyes widened, and he sat back. "What?"

"I am no longer a soldier, but I still have work to do. I must take a copy of the Declaration and the Bounty Resolution to Little Rock to be published. We must build support for the new republic in the States. We need money, supplies, and more men."

William had suddenly spun around and raised his arms and his voice, so the men in the vicinity could see and hear. "What do you say, boys? Will the men of Little Rock send us their support? Let them hear our mighty force!" The exclamation was received with whoops and shouts from the men, and even those who had not heard William took the shouts even further, so the sound traveled past where they could see.

Jesse returned his brother's smile and understood that William was not, this time, accusing him of cowardice, but showing him that he understood their different paths.

"If only those running away could hear," Jesse said, "they would take heart and know that victory would be soon at hand."

William nodded, and the brothers embraced again before going to find some manner of field supper.[13]

11

BADGETT'S LANDING

But several gentlemen who came up from Arkansas, inform us, that the fall of San Antonio, and the massacre of the garrison, is fully confirmed. Only three lives were spared: those of the lady of Lieut. Dickinson, a black servant woman, and a child. Among those who were massacred were, we are informed, Col. Travis (the commanding officer of the post), Col. David Crockett, Col. James Bowie, Col. Jesse Benton, (a brother of one of the senators from Missouri) & c. It is also said, though we believe it is not certain) that Messrs. Charles E Rice, Nathaniel Dennis, and Wm. Badgett, of the place, are among the slain. Col. Crockett, with about 50 resolute volunteers, had cut their way into the garrison, through the Mexican troops, only a few days before the fall the San Antonio.

Jesse had read this passage, printed on the first page of the *Arkansas Gazette* on April 12, 1836, many times since it had been published and kept a clipping of it between the leaves of an unfinished ledger. Sometimes the passage had managed to wrench a wry sort of laugh out of him, and sometimes it did not.

Two days after his return to Little Rock, Jesse saw his copy of the Declaration printed in the April 5, 1836 weekly edition of the *Gazette*. The Bounty Resolution and his account of events in Texas were published in the next weekly edition, an account that was reprinted from paper to paper all the way to the northeast coast, or so he had been told by the *Gazette's* editor some months later.

Jesse's own account of the Alamo and the Convention, which contradicted the first page on several points, was printed on the second and third pages of the same issue. He corrected the report that his brother William and Colonel Jesse Benton had died. He also added his voice, as he would do over and over that Spring, to those who urged Arkansans to look at the new Texas Republic with hope and expectation for a long-term victory rather than with hopelessness in the face of the clear defeats at San Patricio, the Alamo, and Goliad. He told Woodruff of the incoming flood of volunteers that swept him along as they crowded into General Houston's camp. *Instead of [the defeats] disheartening the people,* the editor wrote, *they seem to be inspired with new courage and are rushing to the rescue of their country in such numbers as to give them strong hope of their ultimate success.*

Woodruff did not print Jesse's recollections about the terrified people in their runaway flight up Old San Antonio Road. The trickling exodus of colonists that began when Santa Anna was rumored to be crossing the Rio Grande became a flood with news of the Alamo massacre. Jesse had seen how many of these panicked and poorly-prepared people had died along the way, often buried where they fell. He thought of the image often later in his life—families abandoning their homes to try to survive on the road to an unknown destination.[1]

Noah had been relieved to see Jesse and was greatly relieved to learn that William was not dead as rumored. Over many days and nights, when memory and the need to talk pressed upon him, Jesse told his full story to Noah, including the parts that Woodruff did not print in the *Gazette* and the parts that Jesse did not tell Woodruff. He told Noah about how the smell of the hospital still would not leave his nostrils and how the foolishness of the Provisional Government had left the Alamo without adequate money, provisions, and men. He spoke of how the split command dispute had almost destroyed the

Alamo garrison and of the raw fear on the faces of the settlers who fled Santa Anna.

He trusted Noah to recognize the sacrifice and the price already paid by Texians and to understand that more support for Texas was needed. Jesse was right, and Noah was eager to do his part for Texas, though he could not leave his growing family in Little Rock. Noah chaired a committee of Texian sympathizers to raise money for the new republic. Robertson Childress, an attorney in Little Rock and brother of Convention Delegate George Childress, led a committee that used the Bounty Resolution to recruit soldiers. The men of Little Rock supported both committees because they understood that the Declaration and Constitution would last only if they could be defended in the field.[2]

Stunningly, before the two committees were even formed, Jesse's faith in victory was validated. On April 21, just eighteen days after he arrived back in Little Rock, General Houston's army avenged the Alamo at the Battle of San Jacinto, capturing Santa Anna while scattering the Mexican Army. While it took some time for this news to reach Arkansas, it was met with cheers and hollers of *Remember the Alamo* at the Jeffries Hotel in Little Rock. Jesse was struck by the thought that he would need no help to remember those stone walls and the faces and voices of the men who died to hold them.

Although Texas became a republic and Arkansas became a state in 1836, the next few years were not easy ones for either place. A years-long economic depression in the United States began in early 1837. Noah and his business partner had built a strong retail mercantile business, McLain & Badgett in Little Rock, but it struggled and then closed.[3]

Jesse and his brothers did what they could to make do.

In April 1837, Jesse and Noah found themselves witnesses in the trial of William McKee for the murder of Beauford P. Scott. Jesse did not see the murder but was a witness to a prior act of violence when the defendant struck the deceased with a shovel. The matter between the men had been petty, and the death was a waste. Jesse testified that both men were of good character. He could only shake his head at the loss of life and liberty for no reason.

William came briefly back to Little Rock after the Revolution. In August of 1836, he joined the Arkansas Volunteer Regiment of Mounted Gunmen, where he was elected by the men to the rank of second lieutenant, and his unit mustered at Fort Towson to protect the border.[4]

After his militia enlistment was over, William found that his place was no longer in Little Rock, and he returned to Texas. He obtained a Class I Headright of land for his service during the Revolution, but promptly sold it to investors. He worked with the Third Congress of the Republic of Texas as the Assistant Chief Clerk for the House of Representatives from November 5, 1838 to January 17, 1839. When the term ended, he joined the Austin Volunteers under Captain John Bird and finally found battle against the Comanche on Little River. Jesse and Noah heard of Bird's victory through both report and rumor and hoped that William would visit again when his enlistment expired. Perhaps he would give them more detailed accounts of his role in battles and skirmishes. But William never did return. Eventually, word of his death somewhere near Austin reached the remaining Badgett brothers.[5]

Noah formed a new partnership, also called McLain & Badgett, doing business as a commission and forwarding merchant, and the business provided a broad range of services to planters in the plantation economy. In exchange for a mortgage on land and crops, the partnership could advance credit to a planter and then sell them seed and tools to be delivered to the plantation. After harvest, they could arrange for transportation of the crop to market, the sale of the crop, or for its storage in a warehouse to wait for a higher price. There were sometimes additional profits from the sale of insurance. They arranged sales of home furnishings, clothing, or other goods to a planter and arranged for delivery. They also sold enslaved people. The new business slowly got traction in the recovering economy.[6]

Jesse was employed as their agent. While this work sometimes kept him in town, he was on the road often visiting far-flung plantations and different towns and cities. He enjoyed the travel between destinations. He met with people and had a wealth of stories to tell. As time went on, however, the stories people were most curious about were not those he enjoyed telling. He still loved to talk about the land of Texas—the wild roads he had traveled with such urgency, and the long speeches and debates into the night to finish the constitution before the Mexican Army could overtake them. He found it increasingly difficult to talk about the Alamo and the men he never saw again.[7]

He made enough money for a single man and lived well spending the money in his pockets. Owing more money than he could hope to repay, Jesse did not acquire property in his own name. The years wore on and Jesse's nature continued toward the taciturn.

One of his customers was the Redman family, large landowners in Crittenden County, Arkansas, which lay on the Mississippi River about ten miles from Memphis. Jesse liked the Redmans, who seemed interested in his advice regarding how to get the best prices for their cotton. He proved quickly that he had forgotten nothing about the business of cotton, from growing and baling to shipping.

Jesse started to find reasons to linger in Crittenden County, especially when Mary Ann Redman, an eligible daughter of the family, was around. Mary Ann was a fair, sensible young woman of twenty. Jesse found himself showing off on horseback like a much younger man if he knew Mary Ann was watching from the porch. On these occasions, Mary Ann did not clap or shout her approval, but when his eye would turn to her, she gave him a knowing smile and nod.

As they courted, they took a habit of walking together along a path on her father's land, part of it following along the bank of the Mississippi. Mary Ann was more impressed with his sensible and direct manner than his horsemanship. He chose words carefully and spoke amiably but to the point. He told her of how his family came to Tennessee and how he learned the cotton trade. He also explained how bad luck and bad blood between his family and his uncles had turned his business sour. He told her of his time in Arkansas, his brothers, the frontier, and that horrible winter during which he assisted the emigration of the Choctaw.

And, eventually, he told her of the Alamo. The smell of the hospital, the vote for delegates, and his hard runs to San Felipe and Washington. He told stories of Mr. Gray and Zavala and the floor of the carpentry shop. He recounted the crashing tides of fleeing homefolk and gathering volunteers. And he told her of William.

Mary Ann listened attentively to his stories and asked him gentle questions. One spring day, the sun warm but the breeze chilly off the river, they walked along and Mary Ann's practical mind prompted a new question. "Why did you never return to Texas? Claim the headright, as William did?"

Jesse was quiet for a time. He had been asked before by others and had skirted the question with uncharacteristic half-answers, but he knew such verbal dodging would not impress Mary Ann, who was sharp and a gifted judge of character.

"One hundred and three reasons," he said finally, looking out over the Mississippi, east towards Tennessee. "Along with Maverick, I was the elected voice for one hundred and three men in the creation of a new country that they never were able to live in. Every one of them died fighting or were butchered."

After a moment, Jesse turned to Mary Ann, braced for more questions. He found her nodding as if no other answer would have satisfied her.

Jesse, with nothing in his name but debts, worried that he was not a suitable match for Mary Ann, but she was not to be deterred.[8] In 1843, Mary and Jesse were married in a small ceremony.[9]

Jesse quit his job with Noah and lived with Mary Ann on a cotton plantation, known as Holly Bush, or Badgett's Landing, in Crittenden County about a mile upriver from Redman's Point. The land belonged to his mother-in-law, and his arrangement was much like the deal his own father had with his grandfather, but here he was a welcome son-in-law. He helped Mary's family keep up their land, gin their cotton, and direct their enslaved workers. As he had done in 1827, he erected a cotton gin and remained a subject of King Cotton.[10]

He and Mary began their family with the birth of their first son, Marshall, in 1844.

One day in 1846, Jesse received a letter that called him back to his family in Little Rock, giving the sad news of the death of his brother, Samuel. Of the four Badgett brothers who had moved from Tennessee, Samuel's life had been perhaps both the quietest and the hardest. He kept to his land, trying as much as he could to make a comfortable home for himself and, later, for his wife Elizabeth and their infant daughter. He had no interest in politics or growing his place into a larger hold. Indeed, keeping what he had was difficult. Samuel had for years been unable to pay the taxes on his land in a timely manner. Samuel and his wife Elizabeth had a child in the winter of 1846 who did not live to see the spring. The letter that told Jesse of the child's passing had also reported Samuel's death.

Jesse traveled back to Little Rock to visit with Noah and his mother, to mourn the loss of his brother, and to help however he could with the probate estate. By the time he arrived in Little Rock, however, the small dwelling Samuel shared with his wife, Elizabeth, had burned down, leaving nothing to settle of the estate but the land and the livestock.[11]

Jesse spent some time in Little Rock, but soon he returned to his own growing family at Badgett's Landing.

With his brother put to rest, Jesse saddled his horse and set to the road back to his quiet life in Crittenden County. The road was one he had traveled countless times over his life, and as his horse took it up in an easy canter, Jesse noted how hard-packed it was, how wide, and how smoothed it had become by the passage of horses, feet, and wagons over the years. The road that began as something cut into the wild, pushing its way forth with grit in its wake, was now easing the way for those that came behind it.

AFTERWORD

This book came out of my interest in family history. In the 1990s, I discovered that Jesse was kin and that he was a signer of the Texas Declaration of Independence. This discovery quickly led to the work of Texas historian Louis Wiltz Kemp, who wrote that Jesse "is the most obscure of the signers of the Texas Declaration of Independence." Indeed, Jesse's biography today in the Handbook of Texas On-Line includes only the following:

> *He was born in North Carolina about 1807. With his brother William he enrolled in the Texas army on November 15, 1835. The brothers came from Louisiana to Texas early in December, and Jesse B. Badgett joined the command of William B. Travis at the Alamo by February 1, 1836. The soldiers at the Alamo elected him a delegate to the Convention of 1836, where he was seated on March 1. After signing the Declaration of Independence, he left the convention and returned to his home in Arkansas.*[1]

I took Jesse's obscurity as a challenge. He was my first cousin four times removed, so who better to find his history? Jesse became a hobby.[2]

I collected what facts I could find in books and archives and put the information on a timeline. With the help of my mother, Margaret Padgett Partee, I learned to appreciate and respect the work of genealogists who read through various archives to publish the results for the benefit of amateurs like me. Thank you to the many librarians who helped me. Eventually, I ran out of locally available sources to consult. What I did find was always part of a public record. Other than the letter dated January 14, 1832, which itself is a public record, I found no writing by Jesse and no recollection of Jesse recorded by another except the brief description of his appearance and demeanor at the Convention by a fellow delegate.

My first big break came when I went to Maury County for primary research in its archives. There I found hundreds of original paper case files from the early 1800s that have been preserved for over two centuries, first by the efficient court clerks of Maury County, and now by the professional archivists at the Maury County Archives in Columbia, Tennessee. Jesse's handwritten letter from Washington in the Arkansas Territory was in one file and a host of background details was gleaned from other files. Fleshing out this information took years, and the timeline grew.

My second big break was the internet. I ran Jesse's name through Google and found a little more, mostly derived from public records and published materials not readily available to me in Nashville. One day, I was at the Tennessee State Library and Archives scrolling through microfilmed copies of the *Arkansas Gazette*—and testing how fast I could scroll while still spotting Jesse's name on the screen—when a helpful librarian whispered "Do you know about newspapers.com?" That led to my digital epiphany as I quickly found much more information for the time-line. Thank you, Gibb Baxter!

When I thought that I had enough for a story, I turned the time-line into a biographical article that I submitted for publication in history journals. These journals simply ignored my emails except for a single sympathetic editor who took the time to explain tactfully why the article was not suitable for professional publication and who suggested some other sort of publication instead. I greatly appreciated his advice and took the self-publication route after I retired from the daily practice of law. Thank you, Ryan Schumacher!

Writing the book as creative nonfiction opened an entirely new perspective on Jesse. Writing and re-writing and editing and then more editing led to Jesse as he is presented here. While the timeline approach had assembled Jesse's skeleton, there was no flesh and blood Jesse in that article. The creative part is that flesh and blood. For example, he rode his own horse in Texas because he was compensated for the use of his horse, but whether it was a Morgan or was named Athena is up to creative license. Spoken conversations between the people represented here are meant to be reasonable approximations of conversations that likely occurred. I have tried to ground these creative parts solidly in fact and logical inference. I hope that Jesse and any readers of his story approve of the result. Thank you, Emily Thrash!

Indeed, I received generous help and advice from archivists, librarians, genealogists, professional and amateur historians, friends, and others too numerous to mention here by name. I am grateful to them all. I want, particularly, to thank my wife, Debra Jenkins Partee, and my children for their love and support in reading and commenting on various drafts and for listening to me talk about Jesse and the Texas Revolution.

Jesse barely appears in the public records after 1836, so it is difficult to know how he lived after Texas. While lawsuits show that he worked as an agent for McLain & Badgett, I have found nothing to suggest that he used Texas stories to open doors for his commercial endeavors or for public attention, but human nature suggests that he did.[3] Likewise, there is nothing to suggest that the people of Little Rock (in later years) or Crittenden County or Maury County took any notice of his role in the Texas Revolution. His name pops up, but only as part of the list of persons who signed the Texas Declaration.[4]

One of his last public acts was in 1846 when he ran an advertisement in the *Arkansas Gazette* for a runaway enslaved man named Mordecai. It cannot go unsaid that Jesse was blind to the evils of slavery and the slave trade. He did not extend his ideas of liberty and natural rights to people of color. In this, regrettably, he did not evolve. I sincerely hope that Mordecai kept running and made it to freedom.[5]

The circumstances of his death are undiscovered. I do not know when, where, or how he died. As far as I can tell, Jesse lived out his days in Crittenden County with Mary and their growing family. They had four or five children and may have descendants today, but those records are unclear to me and I have had no contact with a descendant. Since I am not confident of the descendant information, I have not included it here. According to the 1860 Census, their last child was Rueben Badgett born in about 1858. Jesse is not recorded in this census, so he could have died sometime between 1857 and 1860.

The 1860 Census also shows that Mary Ann Redman Badgett had acquired property that she did not have in the 1850 Census. Her real estate was valued at $6,400.00 and her personal estate at $7,400.00, about $444,000.00 total in 2021 dollars. I think that given Jesse's insolvency, her father held titles until Jesse died, then gave the property to Mary Ann. Her "personal estate" was likely persons held in bondage. She is buried in Elmwood Cemetery in Memphis, Tennessee where she lived in her old age.[6]

His resting place has not been found. In 1903, a levee broke at Holly Bush—also known as Badgett's Landing—so his grave and the site of his former home may have been obliterated in the flood. I went looking for it in 2016 but found nothing except agricultural land, a new levee, farm-to-market roads, and a very large muddy river.

Also unknown is what the "B." stands for in his name. Although I think that it was probably "Benton," I have found no proof.

My summary of thoughts about Jesse are these:

He was an active risk-taker who earned his living in many ways, including ways that are repugnant.

He was accepted in high places, associating and working with important, powerful people on significant tasks, but he was not himself a highly placed, important, or powerful person. He served the cause of Texan independence, but he was in Texas for only about four months, arriving after the Revolution started with the Battle of Gonzales and leaving before it ended at the Battle of San Jacinto. In

Texas, he was a capable, serious man at the right time and in the right place to use his skills and experience to make important contributions to the Revolution. He apparently never returned to Texas and, although he served in the Texas Volunteer Army for 91 days, he apparently never applied for or received a headright for his service. Why not return to Texas? Why not claim the land? [7]

Given his short time in Texas, Jesse could be an example of what Marquis James called the "floating population" of adventurers who responded to the excitement of Texas but who did not want to be a Texan. On the other hand, maybe he meant to be a Texan in the beginning, but it was simply too painful for him to remember the Alamo. [8]

NOTES

1. Columbia

1. "Public Member Trees," database, Ancestry.com (https://www.ancestry.com: accessed March 26, 2023), "Partee Jenkins Family Tree" by Albert L. Partee, profile for Benton Badgett (1766-1822, d. Maury County, Tennessee). Benton's paternal grandparents were Roger and Elizabeth Badgett, Granville County, North Carolina Will Book 1, No. 253, 305, and his parents were John and Priscilla Badgett, Granville County, North Carolina Will Book 8, 78.

2. In 1782, North Carolina designated the Cumberland River basin as a military reserve for Revolutionary War veteran land claims. Charles made a claim on October 25, 1783, and 11 years later received a warrant for 5,000 acres. North Carolina Warrant No. 450, November 30, 1794; Edythe Rucker Whitley, *Tennessee Genealogical Records: Records of Early Settlers from State and County Archives*, (Baltimore: Genealogical Publishing Company, Inc., 1981), 150. Thirteen years later, on July 4, 1807, surveyors located his acreage at the mouth of Knob Creek. On April 23, 1808, Charles received a certificate for 5,000 acres from the State of Tennessee. In March 1810, Charles transferred 3,200 of these acres to the heirs of Jesse Benton and to the heirs of Colonel Thomas Hart. *The Democratic Clarion and Tennessee* (Nashville) *Gazette*, March 10, 1810. Jesse Benton's sons include Missouri Senator Thomas Hart Benton and Colonel Jesse Benton.

3. Abner went to Maury County, Tennessee with his father in the winter of 1811. *Beverley Jones v. Charles M. Partee*, Maury County Chancery Court Records (Columbia, Tennessee: Maury County Archives), MSS, Deposition of Abner Partee, September 20, 1834. Jesse's grand uncle Edmund Partee testified that their party arrived at Knob Creek on June 16, 1813. *Jones v. Partee*, MSS, Deposition of Edmund Partee, September 20, 1834. Edythe Rucker Whitley; Marise Parrish Lightfoot, *Let the Drums Roll: Veterans and Patriots of the Revolutionary War who Settled in Maury County*, (Columbia, Tennessee: Maury County Historical Society, 1976), 146-7; Jill K. Garrett, *The Maury Genealogist*, Vol. 3, No. 4, (November 1974): 179.

2. Waverley

1. Benton's date and cause of death are undiscovered; however, his will and probate estate are recorded in *Maury County Will Book B-1*, (Columbia, Tennessee: Maury County Archives), 143; *Book C-1*, 304 and Book E, 27-8.

2. After living and farming on Knob Creek for five years, on July 13, 1818, Benton purchased 100 acres from his father-in-law for $500.00. Maury County Deed Book G-1, (Columbia, Tennessee: Maury County Archives), 319. Indeed, on this same date Charles sold a total of 445 acres to two sons and two sons-in-law for $2,500.00 altogether, about $60,000.00 in 2023 dollars.

3. At his father's estate sale on July 1, 1822, Jesse spent $31.61 to purchase "1 man sadle [sic]," "11 reading books," "1 umberilla [sic] & shot bag," "1 pair of pinchers," and five other illegibly recorded items. *Maury County Will Book C-1*, (Columbia, Tennessee: Maury County Archives), 304 (inventory from estate sale). In 2023 dollars that adds up to $812.78 for a young man aged about 15 years. While Jesse was likely born in 1807, I could not confirm the date "March 7, 1807." Sam Houston Dixon, *The Men Who Made Texas Free* (Houston: Texas Historical Publishing Company, 1924), 343.

4. On October 21, 1822, the Maury County Court of Common Pleas and Quarter Sessions appointed an overseer "of the public road from the ford of the creek at Witherspoon's to the crossroads at Partees." Under this overseer were Jesse and 27 other named men including "all within their bounds [to] work thereon under his direction." *Maury County Will Book B-1*, (Columbia, Tennessee: Maury County Archives), 144.

3. A Land of Opportunity

1. Jesse, Noah, and William arrived in Little Rock in early 1830. Creditors sued Jesse and Noah in Columbia on February 10, 1830, alleging that the two brothers had "left this county for Nashville where they intend to descend the river for the lower country." *Samuel A. Gillespie v. John McManus*, Maury County Chancery Court Records (Columbia, Tennessee: Maury County Archives), MSS, Petition filed February 10, 1830. Also in February 1830, process servers in another lawsuit found neither Noah nor Jesse in Maury County. *Samuel A. Gillespie v. Jesse B. Badgett*, Maury County Chancery Court Records, (Columbia, Tennessee: Maury County Archives), MSS, Sheriff's Return of Service Nulla Bona, February [], 1830. Noah later testified that he was present and had personal knowledge of who lived near the Little Rock steamboat landing in March 1830. *Lytle v. The State*, 17 Ark. 608, 650 (1857). On May 21, 1834, Jesse, Noah, and William Badgett patented 480 acres of land in Pulaski County, Arkansas under the Federal Land Act of 1820, 3 Stat. 566, indicating arrival in Arkansas in about 1830. *Trapnall v. Burton*, 24 Ark. 371 (1866).

2. By July 1831, brothers Jesse, Noah, and William each worked as a store clerk in Little Rock. *Gillespie v. Badgett*, MSS, Deposition of Noah Badgett, July 28, 1831.

3. Jesse and William were in Little Rock on the same day – July 28, 1831 – and witnessed a little spat in a political campaign. *Arkansas* (Little Rock) *Advocate*, July 27, 1831; *Gazette-Extra*, July 28, 1831; *Arkansas* (Little Rock) *Advocate*, August 3, 1831. One scholar has mentioned the incident. Lonnie J. White, *Politics on the Southwestern Frontier: Arkansas Territory, 1819-1836*, (Memphis: Memphis State University Press, 1964), 121. Noah was in Little Rock on the same day and sat for a deposition in a lawsuit filed back in Maury County. *Gillespie v. Badgett*, MSS, Deposition of Noah Badgett, July 28, 1831.

4. "[T]he reigning family in Arkansas was composed almost wholly of Tennesseans." Albert V. Goodpasture, "Andrew Jackson, Tennessee and the Union," *The American Historical Magazine*, vol. 1, no. 3, (July 1896), 217. Indeed, in 1819 several families went together from the Duck River area of Tennessee to the Clear Creek Prairie. Rex W. Strickland, "Miller County, Arkansas Territory, The Frontier that Men Forgot, Chapter 1," *Chronicles of Oklahoma*, vol. 18, no. 1, (March 1940), 33.

5. Noah testified by deposition taken in Columbia and referred to the offending cotton gin as the "Jesse B. Badgett Gin." *Dick, Booker, and Company v. Arkey Y. Partee*, Maury County Circuit Court Records, (Columbia, Tennessee: Maury County Archives), MSS, Deposition of Noah Badgett, August 21, 1832. Dick, Booker bought cotton bales along the Duck River and floated them on flatboats down to New Orleans. *Turney v. Wilson*, 15 Tenn. 340 (1835).

6. Charles S. Aiken, "The Evolution of Cotton Ginning in the Southeastern United States," *Geographical Review*, vol. 63, no. 2 (1973), 196-224.

7. Jesse and his mother Levina Partee Badgett were sued by her brother Archelaus "Arkey" Y. Partee and her father over actual possession of the slave Elsie and her four children, alleging that "their value would not be a satisfaction ... as they [are] family slaves and ... [Arkey is] unwilling to part with [them] for their value." The Badgetts alleged that Charles had given Elsie to Levina after Jesse was born; however, Arkey denied this and claimed ownership by gift for himself. Charles agreed with Arkey. *Charles Partee v. Levina Badgett*, Maury County Chancery Court Records, (Columbia, Tennessee: Maury County Archives), Reel 62, Final Order, February 4, 1828.

8. The partnership of Ackey & Porter sued Jesse for a debt. *National Banner and Nashville Daily Advertiser*, March 25, 1833. On the other hand, Jesse had sued Henry E. Turner in Alabama and won a judgment for $120. *Jesse Badgett v. Henry E. Turner*, Limestone County Circuit Court Minutes 1827-1832, (Athens, Alabama: Limestone County Archives), 25. Turner then sued Jesse's uncle Hiram Partee for indemnity and needed Jesse's testimony as a material witness, but Jesse was in Arkansas. *Henry E. Turner v. Hiram Partee*, Maury County Circuit Court Records, (Columbia, Tennessee: Maury County Archives), MSS, Petition filed October 25, 1831. Jesse also sued to recover the cost of a slave who died shortly after he bought her. *James P. Peters v. James E. Dobbins*, Maury County Chancery Court Records, (Columbia, Tennessee: Maury County Archives), Reel 63, Deposition of Noah Badgett, February 12, 1831. Two other transactions involving Jesse and his slave ownership are recorded in the deed books of Maury County, Tennessee. *Maury County Tennessee Deed Book N-1*, (Columbia, Tennessee: Maury County Archives), 195 (November 27, 1828) and 364 (May 25, 1829).

9. After losing in the trial court, the Badgetts appealed and in the state supreme court, lost again. *Partee v. Badget*, 2 Tenn. 174, 174-5 (1833). Charles died while the appeal was pending and left Elsie and her children to Arkey as a bequest in his will to signal his opinion on who should win the appeal. Will of Charles Partee, *Maury County, Tennessee Will Book X*, (Columbia, Tennessee: Maury County Archives), 81.

10. The details of how Charles sat in bed on October 22, 1828, drinking apple cider and dictating his will to Judge Kennedy come from the transcript of the litigation contesting that will. Charles' notes are preserved in the record. *John E. Brown, Executor v. George Washington Sherman*, Maury County Chancery Court Records, (Columbia, Tennessee: Maury County Archives), Reel 15. His will specifically mentions 1,640 acres and 32 slaves in addition to other unspecified acreage and slaves. Will of Charles Partee, *Maury County, Tennessee Will Book X*, 81. Charles died on December 18, 1829. His death was reported in one newspaper as "Col. Charles Partee died Maury County, Tennessee, veteran of the Revolutionary War." *Jackson* (Tennessee) *Gazette*, January 23, 1830. He disinherited the Shermans and

partially disinherited the Badgetts "because I am satisfied their conduct towards me has not been as respectful and dutiful as I conceive it ought to have been." Marise Parrish Lightfoot, *Let the Drums Roll: Veterans and Patriots of the Revolutionary War who Settled in Maury County*, (Columbia, Tennessee: Maury County Historical Society, 1976), 146-7. The Badgetts and the Shermans contested the will, alleging that Partee was not competent to make it, but they lost in the trial court and lost again on appeal. *Brown v. Sherman*, 2 Tenn. 560, 560-1 (1833). On December 17, 1833, his probate estate was worth $4,912.56, or about $176,000 in 2023 dollars.

11. On January 30, 1828, Arkey alleged that both Levina and Jesse B. Badgett "are in a fair way to become insolvent." *Partee v. Badgett*, Maury County Chancery Court Records, Reel 62, Bill of Complaint, 6. On May 25, 1829, Levina, Jesse, and Noah gave deeds of trust on their land, horses, mules, farm equipment and three slaves to George Washington Sherman to secure payment of loan to them from Sherman. *Maury County Deed Book N-1* (Columbia, Tennessee: Maury County Archives), 364-5. On November 4, 1829, the Badgetts sold their Maury County real estate. *Maury County Deed Book O-1* (Columbia, Tennessee: Maury County Archives), 78; *Gillespie v. Badgett*, Maury County Chancery Court Records, Reel 36; Depositions of Jesse B. Badgett, April 27, 1831, and Levina Badgett, April 29, 1830.

4. The Choctaw Nation

1. Arthur H. DeRosier, Jr., *The Removal of the Choctaw Indians*, (Knoxville: The University of Tennessee Press, 1970), 126.
2. President Andrew Jackson signed the Indian Removal Bill on May 28, 1830, which funded and implemented the treaties requiring the Choctaw to move west of the Mississippi River. DeRosier, *The Removal of the Choctaw Indians*, 126. A document filed in the cotton gin lawsuit states that between September 1831 and February 1832, Jesse was "in some way connected with the removal of the Indians perhaps as a civilian ration dealer in their removal west of the Mississippi ...+ has had no settled residence for that time." *Dick, Booker, and Company v. Partee*, Maury County Circuit Court Records, MSS, Motion filed April 18, 1832.
3. In this letter, Jesse wrote that he had a settlement with buildings located near the Choctaw Line and the Red River about 80 miles from Washington, Arkansas Territory. Eighty miles down the new road to Fort Towson puts Jesse's settlement on the Clear Creek Prairie within a few miles of the fort just north of the Red River. *Dick, Booker, and Company v. Partee*, Maury County Circuit Court Records, MSS, Motion filed April 18, 1832, Letter, Badgett to George Washington Sherman, January 14, 1832; Robin Cole-Jett, *The Red River Valley in Arkansas: Gateway to the Southwest*, (Charleston, South Carolina, The History Press, 2014), 35-41 (Choctaw Removal) and 47-54 (trails and roads).
4. Several contracts are clearly associated with Jesse with two small contracts in his name. Document 512, *Correspondence on the Subject of the Emigration of Indians between 30th November 1831 and 29th December 1833, Vol. 1*, (Washington: Duff Green, 1834): 899-900, 951, 959, 1044-5, and 1052; DeRozier, *The Removal of the Choctaw Indians*, 159.

5. Jesse and the cattle still had a long wait ahead after he dated the letter January 14, 1832. The Choctaw did not leave Little Rock until January 25, 1832, and did not begin to arrive in the Indian Territory until March 1833. *Arkansas* (Little Rock) *Gazette*, January 25, 1832; DeRosier, *The Removal of the Choctaw Indians*, 147.

6. David Folsom was born in 1791 in what became Mississippi in 1817. His father was a Scots Irish trader who married two nieces of a Choctaw chief. Folsom served as a colonel in a Choctaw unit under Andrew Jackson during the War of 1812. After the war, he owned a 150-acre farm, a tavern, and a trading post. He was a slave holder. In 1824 he went to Washington, D.C., as part of the Choctaw delegation that negotiated a treaty with President James Monroe. *Nashville Banner and Nashville* (Tennessee) *Whig*, November 8, 1824; Natchez (Mississippi) *Gazette*, March 26, 1825. Folsom vehemently opposed Removal and helped to form the first constitutional government in the Choctaw Nation. He reluctantly signed the Treaty of Dancing Rabbit Creek, which required the Choctaw to move to the Indian Territory west of the Mississippi River. Cole Cheek, *Mississippi Encyclopedia On-line*, David Folsom, http://mississippiencyclopedia.org/entries/david-folsom/ (accessed May 11, 2023).

7. Jesse's letter is in a court record. Sherman's affidavit states that "he received a letter from said Badgett informing him of his design of leaving Little Rock after a trip to the West of that place in company with migrating Indians." Turner's affidavit states "that in fact [Jesse] had accompanied the migrating Indians and would not return to Little Rock until about a certain period." *Dick, Booker, and Company v. Partee*, Maury County Circuit Court Records, MSS, Motion filed April 18, 1832; Letter, Badgett to George Washington Sherman, January 14, 1832; Affidavit of Henry E. Turner, April 18, 1832, *Turner v. Partee*, Maury County Circuit Court Records, MSS. Washington was an important stop on the Southwest Trail that began in Little Rock and ended in Texas. "Indians removed from the southeastern United States during the Jackson administration were funneled through Washington, AT ...." James L. Haley, *Sam Houston*, (Norman, University of Oklahoma Press, 2002), 102; Muriel H. Wright, "Organization of Counties in the Choctaw and Chickasaw Nations," *Chronicles of Oklahoma*, vol. 8, no. 3 (September 1930), 315. Colonel Folsom led the first party of about 550 Choctaw with 45 "large wagons, with teams of four and six horses and oxen" to meet Jesse in Washington, A.T. *Arkansas* (Little Rock) *Gazette*, November 30, 1831 (at Arkansas Post) and *Arkansas* (Little Rock) *Times and Advocate*, January 4, 1832 (at Little Rock).

5. The Little Rock Debating Society

1. "Jesse B. Badgett and Wm Badgett [were] partners under the style William Badgett & Co." *Weekly Arkansas (Little Rock) Gazette*, December 9 and 26, 1832; January 2, 16, and 23, 1833; February 2, 1846. Litigation confirms that Jesse and William were partners. *James Vance v. Jesse B. Badgett*, Pulaski County Chancery Court Records, Order, April 24, 1840. Money paid by the federal government for the Choctaw Removal "stimulated individual entrepreneurial activity" in the Arkansas Territory. Joseph T. Manzo, "Economic Aspects of Indian Removal," *Southeastern Geographer*, vol. 24, no. 2 (November 1984), 116.

2. In early 1832, Noah formed a partnership called McLain & Badgett with his father-in-law John McLain and advertised new goods for sale "from Philadelphia and New Orleans." *Arkansas* (Little Rock) *Gazette*, April 10, 1833; *Arkansas* (Little Rock) *Advocate*, May 14 and 23, 1832; *McLain & Badgett v. Carson's Executor*, 4 Ark. 164, 164 (1842) (suit for "a quantity of articles" sold). Noah was a Mason in the Western Star Lodge No. 2, *Arkansas* (Little Rock) *Gazette*, June 5, 1839, and a member of the Methodist Church. Horace Jewell, *History of Methodism in Arkansas*, (Little Rock: Press Printing Company, 1892), 307.

3. *Arkansas* (Little Rock) *Gazette*, January 23, February 20, March 13 and 20, and June 26, 1833; March 4, 1834.

4. *Arkansas* (Little Rock) *Gazette*, June 19; July 12; October 2, 9, 16, and 23; November 29; December 4, 18 and 25, 1833; January 1, 8, and 24; February 25; and June 17, 1834.

5. As territorial officers, William was popularly elected but Jesse was appointed. Clarence Edwin Carter, ed., *The Territorial Papers of the United States, Volume XIX, The Territory of Arkansas 1829-1836*, (Washington: The Government Printing Service, 1953), 811, 847; *Arkansas* (Little Rock) *Gazette*, April 3 and August 7, 1833; *Arkansas* (Little Rock) *Advocate*, August 7, 1833. Their colleagues William Field and John P. Field (William's deputy clerk) were nephews and allies of the appointed Territorial Governor John Pope. White, *Politics on the Southwestern Frontier: Arkansas Territory, 1819-1836*, 102, 171. In January 1834, Noah was popularly elected to the Little Rock town council. *Arkansas* (Little Rock) *Gazette*, January 8, 1834. In a field of 10, Noah was the top vote getter.

6. The Badgetts were political supporters of Governor Pope. *Arkansas* (Little Rock) *Gazette*, October 30 and November 6, 1833. They also had other friends in high places. In August 1832, Archibald Yell, served as a presidential appointee in the territorial government. Yell was an attorney, militia colonel, former member of the Tennessee House of Representatives, and a friend and political ally of James K. Polk, who was a resident of Maury County. Yell wrote to Polk from Little Rock and referenced a previous letter written for him by "Mr. Badgett" at a time when Yell was too ill to write. Letter Yell to Polk, August 8, 1832, Herbert Weaver and Paul H. Bergeron, ed., *Correspondence of James K. Polk, Volume II, 1817-1832*, (Nashville: Vanderbilt University Press, 1969). At the least, this indicates that Yell knew and trusted at least one brother as being both his and Polk's friend, perhaps Noah, a fellow Mason. Charles had called Polk "a friend" when appointing him as one the executors of his will; however, Polk declined to serve. Will of Charles Partee, *Maury County, Tennessee Will Book X*, 81. Their uncle Arkey also knew Polk and was active in Democratic politics in Maury County. Letter A.Y. Partee to Polk, October 23, 1829, Weaver and Bergeron, ed., *Correspondence of James K. Polk, Volume II, 1817-1832*. In 1827, one of their Partee cousins had married Robert A. Polk, a cousin of Polk. *Maury County, Tennessee Marriage Register Book 1*, 35. Their brother-in-law George Washington Sherman was a supporter of Polk rival, John Bell. *National Banner and Nashville* (Tennessee) *Whig*, September 21, 1835.

7. Jesse's toast was conspicuous at this meeting to celebrate the American Declaration of Independence. After 13 planned toasts, Governor Pope began the voluntary toasts saluting the Society as "[t]he nursery of the future statesmen and patriots of Arkansas" dedicated to the "the cause of truth and human liberty." The governor was followed by the officers of the Society and three politicians who also lauded the Society and its members before Jesse offered a toast to the Declaration itself.

At the time, Jesse was a sitting Territorial magistrate. *Arkansas* (Little Rock) *Gazette*, July 8, 1834; *Arkansas* (Little Rock) *Advocate*, August 1, 1834 (Robertson Childress, president), March 6, 1835 (Charles E. Rice, secretary), and November 4, 1836 (Society changes its name to the "Lyceum"); Walter Moffatt, "Cultural and Recreational Activities in Pioneer Arkansas," *The Arkansas Historical Quarterly*, vol. 13, no. 4 (1954), 372-85; Walter B. Hendrickson, "Culture in Early Arkansas: The Antiquarian and Natural History Society of Little Rock," *The Arkansas Historical Quarterly*, vol. 17, no. 1 (1958), 31.

8. The *Gazette* reported the death of two-year-old John Oscar Badgett, the "son and only child" of Noah. *Arkansas* (Little Rock) *Gazette*, July 29, 1834.

6. Gone to Texas

1. The circumstances of this business failure suggest that they were not good businessmen. A cascade of lawsuits continued for years, beginning with an action against Jesse. *Arkansas* (Little Rock) *Advocate*, June 5, and July 3, 1835. Litigation shows that the brothers owed at least $4,553.77 (about $156,000.00 in 2023 dollars) and that their creditors were still trying to collect in 1846. *Weekly Arkansas* (Little Rock) *Gazette*, February 2, 1846. When in business, they had four competitors, including McLain & Badgett, *Arkansas* (Little Rock) *Times and Advocate*, May 1, 1835, and the S. Hill & Company quickly opened a new store in their old location. *Arkansas* (Little Rock) *Times and Advocate*, July 3, 1835; *Fowler v. McClelland*, 5 Ark. 188, 188 (1843).

2. *Arkansas* (Little Rock) *Times and Advocate*, April 10, 1835.

3. *National Banner and Nashville* (Tennessee) *Whig*, July 8, 1835.

4. Claude Elliott, "Alabama and the Texas Revolution," *The Southwestern Historical Quarterly*, vol. 50, no. 3 (1947), 315-28.

5. *Arkansas* (Little Rock) *Advocate*, November 6, 1835.

6. *Arkansas* (Little Rock) *Times and Advocate*, November 13, 1835.

7. Louis Wiltz Kemp, Michelle M. Haas, ed., *Our (unlikely) Fathers, The Signers of the Texas Declaration of Independence*, (Houston: Copano Bay Press, 2014), 23-31. At this time, none of the various units of the Volunteer Army had been organized. Eugene C. Barker, "The Texan Revolutionary Army," *The Quarterly of the Texas State Hospital Association*, vol. 9, no. 4 (April 1906), 236-7; *Arkansas* (Little Rock) *Gazette*, July 28, September 8, and November 10, 1835; *Arkansas* (Little Rock) *Advocate*, August 7, 1835. Neither Noah nor Samuel went to Texas. On November 11, 1835, Noah was re-elected as an alderman for the city of Little Rock. Dallas Tabor Herndon, *The Highlights of Arkansas History*, (Little Rock: Arkansas Historical Commission, 1922), 61.

7. The Singular Letter

1. A group of volunteers wrote to the Provisional Government that "Messrs Jesse & W. Badget" had reported to them that 120 United States citizens had left Natchitoches, Louisiana about December 1st and on December 10, 1835, were in Nacogdoches to join the Texian military forces; however, they lacked the financial means to equip themselves and to travel south. The men appealed to the govern-

ment to send an agent with money to defray their costs. The writers noted that the Badgetts were known to Thomas Jefferson Chambers as "men of truth." Wallace O. Chariton, *100 Days in Texas: The Alamo Letters*, (Plano: Wordware Publishing, Inc. 1990), 19-20; Kemp, Haas, ed., *Our (unlikely) Fathers*, 23 fn 3. Chambers was a peripatetic Virginian who grew up in Kentucky, became an attorney in Alabama, and was an appointed judge in Texas under the Mexican Government.

2. Chariton, *100 Days in Texas*, 19-20. This letter is quoted by Kemp. Kemp, Haas, ed., *Our (unlikely) Fathers*, 23.

3. In 1844, Jesse swore that he "saw" Nathaniel Dennis enlist in Nacogdoches on November 15, 1835, and that Dennis later attached himself to "Grant & Johnson's company." *Texas Memorials and Petitions 1834 – 1929*, Petition by Heirs of Nathaniel Dennis, Affidavit of Jesse B. Badgett, March 8, 1844; Kemp, Haas, ed., *Our (unlikely) Fathers*, 23. In a special election on August 3, 1835, Dennis had come in third in a three-way race for constable of Big Rock Township in Pulaski County. *Arkansas* (Little Rock) *Gazette*, August 4, 1835.

4. Charles E. Rice attached himself to the "Matamoras Expedition." *Arkansas* (Little Rock) *Advocate*, April 22, 1836. In January 1835, Rice had become a publishing partner and was named on the masthead of the *Arkansas Advocate* with Albert Pike – who was also editor – before "leaving Little Rock to join the Texas army in November 1835." D. A. Stokes, "The First State Elections in 1836," *The Arkansas Historical Quarterly* 20, no. 2 (1961): 128. Rice was the secretary of the Little Rock Debating Society. *Arkansas* (Little Rock) *Advocate*, January 9, 1835. On October 27, 1835, just days before he left for Texas, Rice was appointed by the Arkansas Legislative Council as a Territorial justice of the peace for Pulaski County. *Arkansas* (Little Rock) *Advocate* October 30, 1835.

5. Grant was likely working for the British Government to keep Texas from joining the United States. Although Houston had posted Neill to command Bexar, Grant stripped the Alamo of men and supplies and left the Alamo on January 1, 1836. Stuart Reid, *The Secret War for Texas*, (College Station, Texas: Texas A&M University Press, 2007), 64-8. Grant's plan may have been to erect a new country composed of Northern Mexican states and to align that country with Great Britain.

6. On January 5, Jesse left the Alamo as an express courier for an 11-day ride to San Felipe de Austin which would have put him back at the Alamo on January 16, 1836. *Republic of Texas Audited Claims*, Jesse B. Badgett, No. 340. (A copy of this expense report is included in this book.) Meanwhile, Frank Johnson was in San Felipe and pressed the General Council for more support of the Matamoros Expedition. Chariton, *100 Days in Texas*, 100-04; John Sutherland, *The Fall of the Alamo*, (San Antonio: The Naylor Company, 1936), 3.

7. On January 5, Jesse bought stationary for the use of the "H. Quarters" at the Alamo. *Republic of Texas Audited Claims*, Jesse B. Badgett, No. 340.

8. On January 3, Jesse bought supplies for the hospital, including 24 bottles of Madera wine and other items which were recorded in an illegible manner. *Republic of Texas Audited Claims*, Jesse B. Badgett, No. 340. There is a difference between Madeira wine from Portugal and Madera wine from Texas. Dr. Amos Pollard reported on December 17, 1835, that the hospital had 16 severely wounded men from the Siege. Chariton, *100 Days in Texas*, 100-04.

9. Dr. Amos Pollard graduated from the medical school at Middlebury College in August 1826. *The National* (Middlebury, Vermont) *Standard*, August 22, 1826. He was a well-known abolitionist who posted from Texas a letter dated February 15, 1835, to William Lloyd Garrison in Boston, Massachusetts. Garrison published the letter in his weekly abolitionist newspaper. *The* (Boston) *Liberator*, May 16, 1835. In the letter, Pollard called for anti-slavery men from New England – "friends of freedom from the free United States" – to move to Texas to enjoy its advantages and to out-vote the pro-slavery men.

10. For about seven years, from 1813 to 1820, Neill and Jesse had lived near each other in Middle Tennessee with the Neills in Bedford County and the Badgetts in Maury County. Their interaction in Tennessee seems doubtful since during this time Jesse was aged six to 13 years while Neill was aged 25 to 32 years, but they certainly may have known some of the same people and places and events. Richard King, *James Clinton Neill, The Shadow Commander of the Alamo*, (Austin: Eakin Press, 2002), 14 - 21.

11. Wallace O. Chariton posits that an undiscovered letter from Neill prompted Governor Smith to dismiss the General Council on January 9, 1836, an act that led to the paralysis of the Provisional Government when the General Council retaliated by impeaching Smith and elevating the lieutenant governor as his replacement. Chariton argues that this singular letter was not among the dispatches forwarded on January 6th by General Houston to Smith, but reached Smith by other means, may not have been an "official" communication intended for the public record, and is now missing or was perhaps destroyed because of its personal and accusatory nature. Moreover, Chariton estimates that the distance between the Alamo and San Felipe could have been covered by a "spirited ride" of three days, but that a more likely time was about four days. Wallace O. Chariton, *Exploring the Alamo Legends*, (Plano: Wordware Publishing, 1990) vi, 107 – 15, 117-30; Todd Hansen, ed., *The Alamo Reader: A Study in History*, (Mechanicsburg, Pennsylvania: Stackpole Books, 2003), 678.

    This previously undiscovered express ride by Jesse, who left the Alamo on January 5 and who certainly could have been in San Felipe by January 8 or 9, is a clear means and opportunity by which such a letter from Neill could have reached Smith in the relevant time frame. Given Jesse's 11-day expense claim, if he spent eight days total travel time, then he had a three-day layover in San Felipe to see the wheels fall off the Provisional Government. Moreover, the great expense of the trip – $2,200.00 in 2023 dollars –indicates that Neill's purpose in sending Jesse was important. Neill relied upon and trusted Jesse to carry out important tasks for the Alamo garrison, including this one. *Republic of Texas Audited Claims*, Jesse B. Badgett, No. 340.

12. Jesse could have stayed in San Felipe for three days to witness real political drama on January 10, 11, and 12 and still have time to return to the Alamo by the sixteenth. On January 9, Governor Smith sent a "Special Call of the House" to the General Council in which he castigated the Council's conduct that he thought was against the best interests of Texas and vowed to govern without the Council until the Convention assembled on March 1, 1836. Chariton, *100 Days in Texas*, 121-23. After having met in secret session on January 10 to consider the governor's message, the Council struck back, going public on January 11 by ordering Governor Smith "to cease the function of his office" and by swearing in the lieu-

tenant governor as the "acting governor." Chariton, *100 Days in Texas*, 126-28. On January 12, the Council published an "Address to the People of Texas" explaining their replacement of Governor Smith, followed by a flurry of communications between Smith and the Council, but no oil was poured upon the waters. Chariton, *100 Days in Texas*, 128-133. By the time that Jesse left San Felipe, the Provisional Government had essentially ceased to function.

8. The Bexar Resolutions

1. On January 16, 1836, Amos Pollard wrote to Governor Smith about the upcoming election in Bexar and the continuing needs of the hospital. Hansen, ed., *The Alamo Reader*, 655; Amelia Williams, "A Critical Study of the Siege of the Alamo and of the Personnel of Its Defenders," *The Southwestern Historical Quarterly*, vol. 36, no. 4 (1933), 270.

2. On January 17, William enrolled with the United States Invincibles and went south toward Copano. Muster Roll of Captain Chenoweth's Company, *Muster Rolls of the Texas Revolution*, (Archives Division, Texas General Land Office, Austin), 68. The Invincibles had been re-organized in late 1835 as a special mounted unit ordered to the gulf port of Copano to secure the area for the Matamoros Expedition. By mid-January 1836, when William joined their ranks, the unit was spread out south from Goliad down the road through Refugio to Copano. Thomas Ricks Lindley, *Alamo Traces: New Evidence and New Conclusions*, (Republic of Texas Press, Lanham, 2003), 49, 53, 74-5 fn 34, 95, 103-4, 208 fn 34). The Invincibles were not under the command of Grant and Johnson. Reid, *The Secret War for Texas*, 95-7.

3. A "patriotic citizen of the United States" loaned $500.00 to the Provisional Government, intending that the money be used "to pay the soldiers in the garrison of Béxar;" however, the General Council spent the money elsewhere. The men at the Alamo were much aggrieved by what they saw as misappropriation. Chariton, *100 Days in Texas*, 172-3; Hansen, ed., *The Alamo Reader*, 663. The benefactor was Henry M. Clay of Alabama. Malcolm D. McLean, ed., *Papers Concerning Robertson's Colony in Texas*, Volume XIII, (Arlington: The University of Texas at Arlington Press, 1987), 275.

4. On January 23, 1836, Neill wrote a letter to Governor Smith requesting a writ of election. Chariton, *100 Days in Texas*, 169; King, *James Clinton Neill*, 92. Davis says that "[o]n January 23 Neill wrote to Smith again asking for a writ of election." William C. Davis, *Three Roads to the Alamo*, (New York City: Harper Collins, 1998), 497.

5. On January 26, 1836, Neill called an indignation meeting and convened a committee to review the $500.00 Loan problem, upon which the garrison wanted to be heard by the Council. Chariton, *100 Days in Texas*, 172-3; King, *James Clinton Neill*, 93; Lindley, *Alamo Traces*, 321; Henry Smith, "Reminiscences of Henry Smith," *The Quarterly of the Texas State Historical Association*, Vol. 14, No. 1 (July 1910), 55-6.

9. The Alamo Delegate

1. On February 1, 1836, election judges used three pages as voter roll / vote tally sheets. These sheets and the Certificate of Election dated February 2, 1836, all

survive. Lindley, *Alamo Traces*, 319-22. The originals are on-line with the Texas State Library and Archives. https://www.tsl.texas.gov/treasures/republic/alamo/election-1.html (accessed March 1, 2023). One writer says that James Butler Bonham was elected instead of Jesse but declined to serve because he preferred "action to deliberation," then Jesse "became" the delegate. Paula Mitchell Marks, *Turn Your Eyes Toward Texas: Pioneers Sam and Mary Maverick*, (Texas A&M University Press, College Station, 1989): 54. I could find no evidence for this scenario; the evidence cited above shows that Jesse was elected over Bonham by 100 votes to 1. After the election, Major Jameson described both Jesse and Maverick as "staunch Independence men & damn any other than such." Chariton, *100 Days in Texas*, 222-3.

2. On February 4, Jesse loaned $50.00 cash to Neill "for pay of the soldiers." *Republic of Texas Audited Claims*, Jesse B. Badgett, No. 340. In a letter dated January 6, 1836, Neill wrote a postscript reminding the Provisional Government that he needed money to pay the "troops who Engaged to Garrison this place for the term of 4 months." These troops "were to be paid monthly and unless money comes in time there are several of them will return home –" Chariton, *100 Days in Texas*, 106. Jesse's loan may have been used by Neill to pay something to keep some of these men at the Alamo. Despite the letter's date of January 6, it seems likely that Jesse carried it when he left the Alamo on January 5.

3. On February 11, 1836, the same day that Neill left the Alamo, he signed Jesse's expense report. *Republic of Texas Audited Claims*, Jesse B. Badgett, No. 340. (A copy of this expense report is included in this book.) At some point, Neill also signed Jesse's honorable discharge from the army to be effective on February 14. *Republic of Texas Audited Claims*, Jesse B. Badgett, No. 321; Chariton, *100 Days in Texas*, 235. This discrepancy could be explained as Neill's post-dating Jesse's discharge so that he served 91 or 92 days (depending upon whether November 15 is counted as day one), at least one day more than needed to obtain a head right of 320 acres for military service. Other soldiers may have been in a similar situation as Neill signed six other discharges to be effective for the same day, February 14. Lindley, *Alamo Traces*, 316 fn 41. Lindley makes the case that Neill signed the discharges when he was back at the Alamo on February 14 to settle the command dispute, Lindley, *Alamo Traces*, 309-10; however, these discharges could easily have been post-dated.

4. On February 17, 1836, Blair's assignment to Jesse was counter-signed by "W.B. Travis, Lt. Col. Cavalry," who commanded the Alamo in Neill's absence. *Republic of Texas Audited Claims*, Jesse B. Badgett, No. 350; Assignment, Samuel C. Blair to Jesse B. Badgett, February 17, 1836 (A copy of this assignment is included in this book.). It is only in Jesse's newspaper account of the Revolution that Blair is identified as being from "Conway county [sic], A [rkansas].T[erritory]," suggesting that they may have known each other before the Alamo. In addition, the account identifies Major Jameson as being from Kentucky, which may also reflect Jesse's knowledge of that officer. *Arkansas* (Little Rock) *Gazette*, April 12, 1836.

5. When Jesse rode out of the Alamo, he left two bottles of wine "for the use of the hospital" and three pounds of gunpowder "for the use of the garrison." On February 17, 1836, when Travis counter-signed Blair's assignment, he also signed a receipt for these items, requesting that the Provisional Government pay Jesse $3.87 ½ as reimbursement. *Republic of Texas Audited Claims*, Jesse B. Badgett, No. 340;

Chariton, *100 Days in Texas*, 243. Colonel Travis also claimed on an expense for February 17. In a footnote, William C. Davis addresses the puzzle of how Travis' red leather account book – with its last entry on February 17 – survived the fall of the Alamo and concludes that "it seems ... likely that Travis sent it out himself, hoping for a speedy reimbursement." Davis, *Three Roads to the Alamo*, 526 fn 92. Travis could easily have given it to Jesse on February 17 to take to the Convention.

6. On February 29, 1836, when Jesse was in Washington, Texas his brother was within a day's ride of the Alamo. William had been on the road since he left Béxar with the Invincibles about January 17, 1836. On February 1, he had been an election judge for the army vote in Refugio. Kemp, Haas, ed., *Our (unlikely) Fathers*, 300. On February 26, William was in Goliad with other mounted men under Captain Chenoweth, Lindley, *Alamo Traces*, 103-4, when Colonel Fannin sent Chenoweth's command ahead of the main army up the Old Goliad Road toward the Alamo to the Sequin Ranch on the San Antonio River about 33 miles southeast of the fort. This group was the vanguard of Fannin's relief force for the Alamo. At the ranch with Chenoweth, William collected corn, cattle, and hogs for Fannin's later use and fell back to hold the Cibolo River crossing on the Old Goliad Road. Lindley, *Alamo Traces*, 123-4, 127-8, 142, 208 fn 34; Jesus F. de la Teja, ed., *A Revolution Remembered: The Memoirs and Selected Correspondence of Juan N. Sequin*, (Austin, Texas: Texas State Historical Association: 2002), 78-80 (Sequin Ranch foraged on February 28).

7. Zavala served in the Spanish Cortes before he became a "hero of the revolution that had won freedom from Spain" in 1821. He was a delegate to the Mexican Constitutional Convention and opposed Santa Anna's abrogation of the resulting Constitution of 1824. He held several offices under various Mexican governments including governor, senator, and cabinet officer. On August 39, 1834, he resigned as Minister to France to protest Santa Anna's dissolution of Congress and settled in Texas upon his return. At the Consultation of 1835, Zavala was the "most striking figure present." Marquis James, *The Raven, A Biography of Sam Houston*, (Indianapolis: The Bobbs Merrill Company, 1929): 214. At the Convention in 1836, Zavala's "polished manners, dark complexion, and foreign tongue were never to endear him to the rank and file of the Anglo-Saxon settlers who had preceded him, but his knowledge, experience, and ability were to render him almost indispensable" to Texas. Raymond Estep, "Lorenzo de Zavala and the Texas Revolution," *The Southwestern Historical Quarterly*, vol. 57, no. 3 (January 1954), 322, 332. One observer found Zavala to be "the most interesting man in Texas." William Fairfax Gray, *Diary of Col. Wm. F. Gray, Giving Details of His Journey to Texas and Return in 1835-1836 and Second Journey to Texas in 1837*, (Houston: The Fletcher Young Publishing Company, 1965), 120.

8. On Monday, February 29, 1836, the day before the Convention began, Jesse received his military pay and was reimbursed for his expenses and loans. *Republic of Texas Audited Claims*, Jesse B. Badgett, Nos. 321 (military services), 332 (military services), 340 (Alamo expenses), and 350 (Blair assignment).

9. On February 1, 1836, from a field of 17 candidates, the Municipality of Béxar elected the top four vote getters to the Convention: Navarro (65), Ruis (61), Captain Juan Nepomuceno Seguín (60), and Don José Gaspar Flores de Abrego (59). Although the soldiers could not vote in the municipal election, the bottom four vote getters were soldiers: Jesse (3), Pollard (2), Maverick (2), and Bonham (1).

Hansen, ed., *The Alamo Reader*, 602-4. Although Sequin and Gaspar had both served on the Béxar Resolutions committee with Jesse; they did not attend the Convention as Jesse and Maverick filled their positions for the Municipality after receiving an almost unanimous vote at the Alamo. Neill wrote to Houston that "I can say to you with Confidence that we can rely on great aid from the Citizens of this town in case of an attack. They have no money here, but Don Jasper Flores, and [] Navaro [sic], have offered us all their goods Groceries, and Beeves." Hansen, ed., *The Alamo Reader*, 652; David R. McDonald and Timothy M. Matovina, ed., *Jose Antonio Navarro Defending Mexican Valor in Texas*, (Austin, Texas: State House Press, 1995), 74-6. These facts reflect an apparently successful political bargain between a town and a fort with common objectives.

10. On Tuesday, March 1, 1836, the Convention organized itself; Jesse submitted his credentials and was seated for the Municipality of Béxar along with Ruis and Navarro. *Journal of the General Convention at Washington, March 1-17, 1836*, (Houston, 1838), 3-6; Gray, *Diary of Col. Wm. F. Gray*, 121-3; Hansen, ed., *The Alamo Reader*, 670-1 (Jesse's credentials). A fellow delegate described Jesse as "a man of large and muscular frame and wore a full beard which was dark, as was the hair of his head. He was not a man of many words, but when addressed he always responded cordially." Dixon, *The Men Who Made Texas Free*, 344. At least one other delegate – Augustine Blackburn Hardin (1807 – 25) – had also lived in Maury County, Tennessee at the same time as Jesse (1813 – 30). Dixon, *The Men Who Made Texas Free*, 289. On this day, there was a peaceful transfer of power from the Provisional Government to the Convention.

11. On Wednesday, March 2, the delegates agreed to a declaration of independence from Mexico. *Journal of the General Convention*, 6-17; Gray, *Diary of Col. Wm. F. Gray*, 123-4. Pandemonium followed during which "General Houston stood on a bench in the midst of the boisterous delegates and cried out, "Gentlemen, one word! Let us pledge ourselves to remain in Washington until we complete our labors." Dixon, *The Men Who Made Texas Free*, 260. Also on March 2, Jesse wrote a letter to his brother Noah in Little Rock and told of his election to the Convention and William's continued service in the revolutionary army. This letter was reported in a Little Rock newspaper with little detail. *Little Rock* (Arkansas) *Times*, April 4, 1836. The letter itself has not been discovered.

10. The Call and the Fall

1. On Thursday, March 3, 1836, the delegates signed the declaration without fanfare and Jesse was appointed to a military affairs committee. *Journal of the General Convention*, 18-21; Gray, *Diary of Col. Wm. F. Gray*, 124. A 1936 painting by Charles and Fanny Normann, entitled "The Reading of the Texas Declaration of Independence" depicts Jesse on the far-right side of the frame standing tall and somewhat alone beside a window, wearing buckskin and sporting a heavy mane of black hair and full beard. R. Henderson Shuffler, "The Signing of Texas' Declaration of Independence: Myth and Record," *The Southwestern Historical Quarterly*, Vol. 37, No. 3, (January 1934): 312, 330. Buckskin Jesse was likely influenced by the description of him as having grown up hunting and fishing in the wilds of Arkansas and a fellow

delegate's description of his physique and demeanor. Dixon, *The Men Who Made Texas Free*, 343.

2. On Friday, March 4, the Convention appointed Sam Houston commander of the military. *Journal of the General Convention*, 55-62; Gray, *Diary of Col. Wm. F. Gray*, 124.

3. On Sunday, March 6, the Convention received this call to arms from Travis and Maverick took his seat. *Journal of the General Convention*, 25-8; Gray, *Diary of Col. Wm. F. Gray*, 125-6. Travis wrote the call on February 24, 1836, the day after the Siege began, but it took 11 days to reach the Convention. Chariton, *100 Days in Texas*, 267. Lindley wrote that Travis' message "is admired as the paramount expression of American sacrifice in a combat situation." Lindley, *Alamo Traces*, 97. After the call was read, a "painful silence prevailed for a brief period," then "great excitement prevailed and a movement was started to adjourn the convention and go to Travis' rescue." Houston "spoke with great eloquence and fervor" against adjournment, vowed to leave himself to command the army, and urged the other delegates to stay. "Tumultuous applause followed," and as Houston left and the others remained. Dixon, *The Men Who Made Texas Free*, 95, 163-4, 296.

4. On Monday, March 7, the delegates worked on a constitution and other essential tasks of governing. *Journal of the General Convention*, 28-33; Gray, *Diary of Col. Wm. F. Gray*, 126.

5. On Tuesday, March 8, the Convention sent Jesse to collect records from the Provisional Government. He was a good choice as a relative neutral in Texian politics who had met Governor Smith and others in that government when he was in San Felipe. *Journal of the General Convention*, 33-9; Gray, *Diary of Col. Wm. F. Gray*, 126-7.

6. On Wednesday, March 9, the Convention worked on the Constitution and Jesse moved into the carpentry shop with Gray, Zavala, Navarro, and Ruis. They shared costs equally. *Journal of the General Convention*, 39-54; Gray, *Diary of Col. Wm. F. Gray*, 127-8.

7. On Tuesday, March 15, the delegates learned that the Alamo had fallen on March 6, *Journal of the General Convention*, 75-80; Gray, *Diary of Col. Wm. F. Gray*, 130-1; ironically, the same date on which the Convention had received Travis' call to arms. One delegate noted that "our situation is very bad today we finish the Constitution hurry through the rest of the business, and prepare for desperate efforts." Roy S. Newsom, Jr. and James B. Collinsworth, Jr., *Too Good To Be True: James Collinsworth and the Birth of Texas*, (Kingston Springs, Tennessee: Westview, Inc., 1912), 71.

8. On Wednesday, March 16, the delegates worked through a long night and into the early morning to adopt a constitution and to organize the Convention's successor government, the Ad Interim Government. *Journal of the General Convention*, 80-2; Gray, *Diary of Col. Wm. F. Gray*, 131-3. The Section 9 of the General Provisions of this constitution made slavery legal and defined the status of the enslaved and people of color as being non-citizens with no rights. The Convention did not adjourn until the early morning hours of the seventeenth.

9. On Thursday, March 17, after taking a short break, the delegates reconvened and peacefully transferred power to the Ad Interim Government before adjourning *sine die. Journal of the General Convention*, 82-4; Gray, *Diary of Col. Wm. F. Gray*, 133-5. Jesse may not have left right away and got separated from his house mates because he needed copies of the Declaration and the Bounty Resolution both of

which were later published in the Little Rock newspapers. *Arkansas* (Little Rock) *Gazette*, April 12, 1836; *Arkansas* (Little Rock) *Advocate*, April 15, 1836. The Bounty Resolution had passed on March 14. *Journal of the General Convention*, 75-80. This begs the question, where are the copies that Jesse took to Arkansas?

10. On Friday, March 18, Jesse left Washington, caught up with the others on the road, and spent the night at Groce's Retreat. Gray, *Diary of Col. Wm. F. Gray*, 135-6; *Arkansas* (Little Rock) *Gazette*, April 12, 1836; *Arkansas* (Little Rock) *Advocate*, April 15, 1836. That night, Groce's Retreat was the temporary seat of government for the new Republic of Texas.

11. Jesse told the newspapers in Little Rock that Dennis and Rice died with "Col. Johnson." *Arkansas* (Little Rock) *Gazette*, April 12, 1836; *Arkansas* (Little Rock) *Advocate*, April 15, 1836.

12. Jesse told the newspapers in Little Rock that Crockett had led a party from the Alamo to the Cibolo River crossing, a story that he must have heard from his brother William who was at the crossing with Chenoweth. *Arkansas* (Little Rock) *Gazette*, April 12, 1836. Of the 18 men on the muster roll of the United States Invincibles, 15 are recorded as having been "killed" during the Revolution, excepting only Captain Chenoweth, William Badgett, and J.D. Elliott. Muster Roll of Captain Chenoweth's Company, *Muster Rolls of the Texas Revolution*, 68. A different list of survivors includes Chenoweth and three other men, but not William. Lindley, *Alamo Traces*, 127-8, 134-5, 138, 140-5, 148-51.

13. Jesse told the newspapers in Little Rock that on Saturday, March 19, he found his brother William alive "at General Houston's camp, at Beeson's Crossing of the Colorado" south of Washington. The papers erroneously reported that Jesse returned to the Convention on March 20 until its adjournment on March 22. *Arkansas* (Little Rock) *Gazette*, April 12, 1836; *Arkansas* (Little Rock) *Advocate*, April 15, 1836. In fact, the Convention had adjourned *sine die* on March 17. It seems most likely that Jesse left Beeson's Landing on or about March 20 as he was reported near Nacogdoches on the 25th.

11. Badgett's Landing

1. On Sunday, April 3, 1836, Jesse arrived in Little Rock having passed through Nacogdoches on November 25 and Natchitoches on November 30. *Arkansas* (Little Rock) *Gazette*, April 5, 1836. He gave interviews to the newspapers in Little Rock which published the Declaration and the Bounty Resolution. *Arkansas* (Little Rock) *Gazette*, April 12, 1836; *Arkansas* (Little Rock) *Times and Advocate*, April 15, 1835. Jesse's account was widely published in the spring of 1836. *See, e.g.*, *National* (Washington City) *Intelligencer*, May 3, 1836; *The New Yorker*, May 7, 1836; *Fayetteville* (North Carolina) *Weekly Observer*, May 12, 1836.

2. In April of 1836, a "Texas Meeting" was held to show support for the Texas Revolution. Noah served on a committee to raise men and Childress on a committee to help them get to Texas. *Arkansas* (Little Rock) *Gazette*, April 26, 1836. Such meetings were held in other states as well. *See, e.g.*, James E. Winston, "Mississippi and the Independence of Texas," *The Southwestern Historical Quarterly*, Vol. 21, No. 1, (July 1917), 38-9. Jesse likely also brought with him an advertisement that offered a $50.00 reward for the return of a horse stolen from "Geo. C. Childress" at the "falls

of Brazos" north of Washington, Texas. If found, then George wanted the horse returned to "Col. R. Childress," his brother in Little Rock. *Arkansas* (Little Rock) *Gazette*, April 12, 1836.

3. This economic crash is now known as the Panic of 1837. In May 1837, McLain & Badgett closed its doors and dissolved as a partnership. *Arkansas* (Little Rock) *Times and Advocate*, May 8, 1837; Ted R. Worley, "Arkansas and the Money Crisis of 1836-1837," *The Journal of Southern History*, vol. 15, no. 2 (May 1949), 191.

4. On October 25, 1836, William was a first lieutenant and Robertson Childress was the Adjutant. *Arkansas* (Little Rock) *Gazette*, October 7 and 25, 1836; "Commissioned Officers of the Post," Fort Towson, September 1836.

5. William worked as an assistant clerk in the Texas congress. *Vermont State Paper*, December 7, 1838; *Macon* (Georgia) *Intelligencer*, December 19, 1838; *Republic of Texas Audited Claims*, William Badgett, Nos. 892, 1285, 1355, 1501, 1547, 1627, 1679, 1833, 2808, and one unnumbered receipt (all clerk salary receipts). He was briefly a Texas Ranger under Captain William Bird. Stephen L. Moore, *Savage Frontier Volume II 1838-1839: Rangers, Riflemen, and Indian Wars in Texas* (Denton, Texas: 2006), 217, 220-1. The Texas Rangers is a civil law enforcement agency, not military. Captain Bird and four other Rangers who died in this battle are remembered as losing their lives in the line of law enforcement duty. Houston *Telegraph*, June 5, 1839; Charles M. Robinson, III, *The Men Who Wear the Star: The Story of the Texas Rangers*, (New York: Modern Library, 2000), 50-52. William died without having children. *Trapnall v. Burton*, 24 Ark. 371, 376 (1866).

6. In May of 1838, a new McLain & Badgett partnership opened; but, in 1843 John McLain died. *Arkansas* (Little Rock) *Times and Advocate*, May 8, 1838. *Weekly Arkansas* (Little Rock) *Gazette*, January 26, 1842 ("highest cash paid for Cotton, Peltries and Beef Hides" and "Negroes of either sex from 15 -20 yrs"); *Arkansas* (Little Rock) *Gazette*, November 24, 1841 and October 5, 1842; *Weekly Arkansas* (Little Rock) *Gazette*, February 15, 1843; *Ex Parte Badgett*, 6 Ark. 280, 281 (1845) (business dispute); *Lawson v. Badgett*, 20 Ark. 195, 196 (1859) (business dispute); *Trapnall v. Burton*, 24 Ark. 371, 376 (1866) (business dispute). By 1850, Jesse's mother Lavinia Badgett and two young Sherman grandchildren were living with Noah on his plantation in the Black Rock Township of Pulaski County, 1850 Census, Pulaski County, Arkansas, located "down the river below Little Rock," *Carroll v. Wilson*, 22 Ark. 32, 41 (1860).

7. The facts address actions of "their agent, Jesse B. Badgett." *McLain & Badgett v. Coulter*, 5 Ark. 13, 13 (1843).

8. Jesse was hopelessly insolvent. In 1840, he was ordered to pay $4,550 on a joint debt with the likewise insolvent probate Estate of William Badgett. *James Vance v. Jesse B. Badgett*, Pulaski County Chancery Court Order (April 24, 1840). Creditors sought payment for years. *Cummins v. McLain & Badgett*, 3 Ark. 397, 398 (1840); *Arkansas* (Little Rock) *Gazette*, February 2 and 16, 1846. In 1846, a creditor foreclosed on a mortgage from 1838 when Jesse and William secured extensions of credit on their debt. *Trapnall v. Burton*, 24 Ark. 371, 375 (1866). Another lawsuit resulted in a sheriff's sale of Jesse's interest in 78 acres of land near the Arsenal in Little Rock. *Weekly Arkansas* (Little Rock) *Gazette*, May 8, 1844. There had been litigation over the disputed title. *Weekly Arkansas* (Little Rock) *Gazette*, December 22, 1841. The court also foreclosed on other land mortgaged to pay the partnership debt. *Weekly Arkansas* (Little Rock) *Gazette*, June 30, 1845, February 2 and 16, 1846.

Lawyers in Maury County contacted lawyers in Little Rock looking for help to collect debts owed in Tennessee. *Jane H.Y. Greenfield v. Thomas G.T. Greenfield*, Maury County Chancery Records, (Columbia, Tennessee: Maury County Archives), Reel 38, Letter Jane H.Y. Greenfield to the Court, August 1847; *Evan Young v. Mary O. Walker*, Maury County Chancery Records, (Columbia, Tennessee: Maury County Archives), Reel 85.

9. No record has been found for Jesse's marriage; however, the 1850 Census shows that Jesse and Mary lived with their six-year-old son named Marshall suggesting a marriage in about 1842 to 1844. 1850 Census, Crittenden County, Arkansas. Although Mrs. Badgett's name is recorded as "Margaret" in the 1850 Census, all other known sources record her name as "Mary Ann." 1860 Census, Crittenden County, Arkansas ("Mary A. Badgett"); *Crittenden County, Arkansas Deed Book E*, 9-10 ("Jesse B. Badgett and Mary Ann his wife"); *Deed Book M*, 476 ("Mary A. Badgett"); *Crittenden County, Arkansas Chancery Court Record Book F*, 333-34 ("Mary A. Badgett"). Mamie Thompson, who was formerly enslaved by the Redman family, remembered in 1937 that after her father died, "Miss Mary married Mr. Badgett" and "they lived in Crittenden County, Arkansas." *Slave Narratives: A Folk History of Slavery in the United States from Interviews with Former Slaves, Volume II, Arkansas Narratives, Part 6*, (Washington, D.C.: Federal Writers Project, 1941), 318-20. They may have been Episcopalian as Jesse donated to that church in Little Rock. Ellen Maria Cantrell, ed., *The Annals of Christ Church Parish from A.D. 1839 to A.D. 1899*, (Little Rock: Arkansas Democrat Company, 1900), 9. Mary is buried in Elmwood Cemetery, Memphis, Tennessee.

10. Badgett's Landing, later known as Holly Bush, was at Mississippi River Mile 744.4. Redman's Landing was located at River Mile 743.4. Frank M. Cayton, *Landings on All the Western and Southern Rivers and Bayous: Showing Locations, Post Offices, Distances, & c.*, (St. Louis: Woodward, Tienon, & Hale Printers and Binders, 1881), 7; Marion Bragg, *Historic Names and Places on the Lower Mississippi River*, (Vicksburg, Mississippi River Commission, 1977), 74. When a fire destroyed "Badgett's cotton gin" at Badgett's Landing on February 12, 1878, Jesse had been dead for about 20 years. Whether Jesse or his son George Redman (G.R.) Redman built the gin, is unknown. *Memphis (Tennessee) Daily Appeal*, February 14, 1878.

11. In 1843, Samuel's 40 acre farm was subject to sale for delinquent taxes. *The (Little Rock) Arkansas Banner*, October 7, 1843. In about 1845, Samuel married Elizabeth, but no record of their marriage has been discovered and her maiden name is unknown. In February 1846, he owned two slaves named Andrew and Jackson, both of whom ran away from this farm located about eight miles south of Little Rock. *Weekly (Little Rock) Arkansas Gazette*, February 9, 1846. His death about that same time is shown by his probate estate sale, which included a male and a female slave. *Weekly (Little Rock) Arkansas Gazette*, March 16, 1846. Before the sale could take place, a fire that started in the smoke house destroyed all buildings and the property inside. *Weekly (Little Rock) Arkansas Gazette*, April 13, 1846. His only child, a daughter name Ophelia, died May 9, 1846.

Afterword

1. Kemp, Haas, ed., *Our (unlikely) Fathers*, 23-31; Dixon, *The Men Who Made Texas Free*, 343-45; L.W. Kemp, "Badgett, Jesse B.," *Handbook of Texas Online,* accessed April 03, 2023, https://www.tshaonline.org/handbook/entries/badgett-jesse-b; published by the Texas State Historical Association.

2. Charles Marion Heiskell, who fought and died at the Alamo, was my first cousin, five times removed on my mother's side of the family.

3. On October 29, 1839, Jesse and Noah were among the named sponsors of a public dinner for the sitting Vice-President of the United States, Richard M. Johnson. *Weekly Arkansas* (Little Rock*) Gazette,* November 6, 1839. Other sightings of Jesse include the following: *Arkansas* (Little Rock) *Gazette,* May 2, 1837 (murder trial); *Arkansas* (Little Rock) *Times and Advocate,* November 22, 1841 and June 12, 1843 (administrator of estate in Conway County); *Arkansas* (Little Rock) *Banner,* June 5, 1844 (administrator of estate in Pulaski County); *Johnston v. Ashley,* 7 Ark. 470, 473-4 (1847) (dispute over a slave); *Arkansas* (Little Rock) *Gazette,* September 25, 1844 (borrowed money); *Weekly Arkansas* (Little Rock) *Gazette,* June 16, 1845 (valued a horse). In January 1853 Jesse administered a probate estate in Crittenden County that was reviewed by the Supreme Court of Arkansas. *Wilson v. Harris,* 13 Ark. 559, 561 (1853). His wife was a Harris heir.

4. Two other Alamo defenders – Asa Walker and Jacob Walker – were also from Maury County, Tennessee. Depending upon which of two stories is true, either Asa or Jacob was the last defender to be killed. Asa wrote a letter with his apology for taking with him to Texas an "overcoat and gun" that were not his to take. Robert W. Ikard, M.D., "The Walker Boys: Were Maury Countians at the Alamo," *Tennessee Historical Quarterly,* vol. 51 no. 4 (Winter 1992), 191-6. An excellent book on the history of Crittenden County, Arkansas makes no mention of Jesse, which underscores how quietly Jesse lived after Texas. Margaret E. Woolfolk, *A History of Marion,* (Margaret E. Woolfolk: 1983).

5. Jesse advertised in Little Rock because he thought that Mordecai would go back to that place from Crittenden County. *Arkansas* (Little Rock) *Democrat,* September 25, 1846, *Arkansas* (Little Rock) *Gazette,* October 4, 1846.

6. 1850 Census, Crittenden County, Arkansas; 1860 Census, Crittenden County, Arkansas; *Crittenden County, Arkansas Deed Book E,* 9 -10.

7. Marks wrote that Maverick "felt a sense of guilt at having survived the Alamo slaughter." Marks, *Turn Your Eyes Toward Texas,* 62.

8. Marquis James, *The Raven, A Biography of Sam Houston,* (Indianapolis, 1929), 281-4.